THE COMPLETE toddler COOKBOOK

101 Easy-To-Make Toddler Meals Everyone Can Eat

Lisa Dauphin

HHF PRESS

SAN FRANCISCO

COPYRIGHT © 2021 HHF Press

First published 2021

All rights reserved. No part of this book may be reproduced in any form or by any electronic or mechanical means, including information storage and retrieval systems, without permission in writing from the publisher, except by reviewers, who may quote brief passages in a review.

Editor: HHF Press

Art Direction: HHF Press

Illustrations: HHF Press

All photographs in this book © Shutterstock.com or © Depositphotos.com

Published in the United States of America by HHF Press

268 Bush St, #3042

San Francisco, CA 94104 USA

www.hhfpress.com

Disclaimer:

Although the publisher and authors of this book are practically obsessed with modern cooking techniques, neither the publisher nor the authors represent or are affiliated with any of the brands mentioned in this text.

All content herein represents the authors' own experiences and opinions, and do not represent medical or health advice. The responsibility for the consequences of your actions, including your use or misuse of any suggestion or procedure described in this book lies not with the authors, publisher or distributors of this book. We recommend using common sense and consulting with a licensed health professional before changing your diet or exercise. The authors or the publisher do not assume any liability for the use of or inability to use any or all of the information contained in this book, nor do the authors or publisher accept responsibility for any type of loss or damage that may be experienced by the user as the result of activities occurring from the use of any information in this book. Use the information responsibly and at your own risk.

The authors and publisher reserve the right to make changes he or she deems required to future versions of the publication to maintain accuracy.

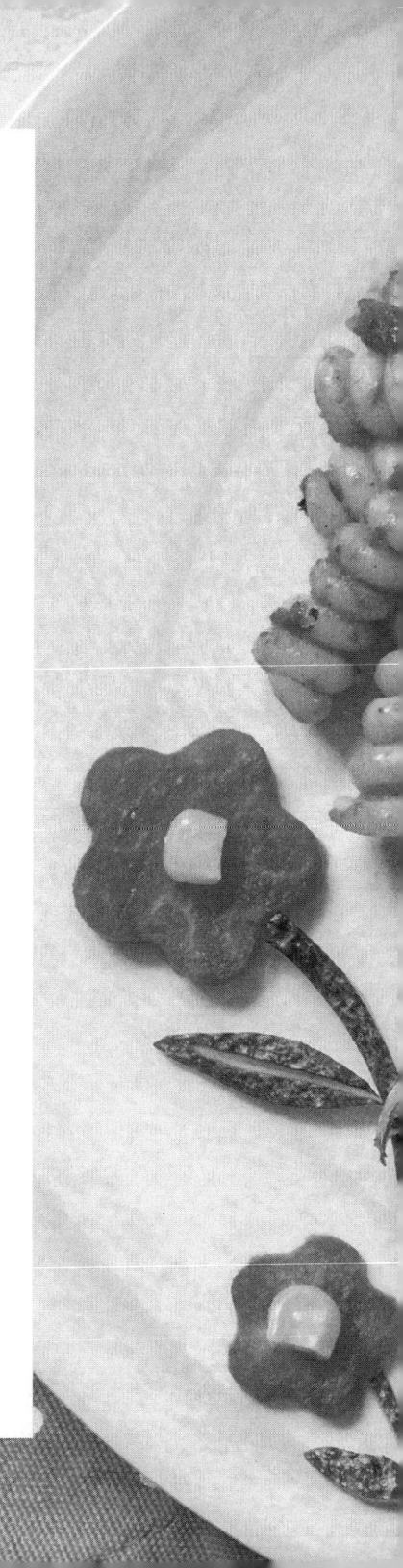

CONTENTS

INTRODUCTION 7

BENEFITS OF COOKING FOR YOUR TODDLER 9

WHAT YOUR TODDLER SHOULD BE EATING 13

MAKE FOOD FOR THE WHOLE FAMILY 21

GETTING THE RIGHT NUTRITION 25

SOLVING A FEW PROBLEMS 31

BREAKFAST FOR THE WHOLE FAMILY 35

- Tasty Breakfast Salad 36
- Breakfast Casserole 38
- Vegetarian Breakfast Tostadas 39
- Broccoli and Cheese Mini Quiches 40
- Veggie Frittata 41
- Weekday Breakfast Burritos 42
- Roasted Veggie Hash 44
- Strawberry and Hidden Veg Smoothie 45
- Spinach and Banana Blender Muffins 46
- Peanut Butter and Banana Wraps 47
- Zucchini Oatmeal Balls 48
- Strawberry Quinoa Breakfast Bowl 49
- Zucchini Pancakes 50
- Breakfast Sausage Patties 52
- Crispy Ham and Cheese Waffles 53

LUNCHTIME AND SNACKS 55

- Chili Mac and Cheese 56
- Easy Spinach Pesto and Pasta 57
- Cheesy Bean Quesadillas 58

- Quinoa Chicken Strips 60
- Crispy Bacon Pasta Salad 61
- Turkey Roll-ups 62
- Homemade Fish Fingers 63
- Make-it-Yourself Sushi 64
- Mini Muffins with a Difference 65
- Roasted Broccoli and Cheese Toastie 66
- Chicken and Quinoa Meaty Muffins 67
- Cheesy Meatball Frittata 68
- Tuna Bean Jacket Potatoes 69
- Creamy Chickpea Curry 70
- Gluten Free Granola Bars 72
- Veggie Stacks 73
- Strawberry Rolls 74
- Baked Cinnamon and Apple Rings 75
- Shaped Crackers 76
- Pizza with a Difference 77
- Mozzarella Sticks 78
- Sweet Potato Chips 79
- Carrot and Apple Oatcakes 80
- Sweet Potato & Peanut Butter Muffins 81
- Tropical Cookies 82

VEGGIES AND SIDE DISHES 85
- Roasted Broccoli 86
- Tasty Oven Cooked Asparagus 88
- Parmesan Roasted Cauliflower 89
- Cauliflower Salad 90
- Easy Glazed Carrots 91
- Zucchini and Baguette Crouton Salad 92
- Italian Baked Sweet Potato 93
- Sweet and Buttery Butternut Squash 94
- Roast Mixed Veggies 95
- Mini Stuffed Tomatoes 96
- Butternut Squash Patties 98
- Quinoa and Herb Salad 99
- Eggplant No-fry Fries 100
- Simple Slaw 101
- Stuffed Baby Portobellos 102
- Crispy Greens 103

DINNER 105
- Meat and Veggie Balls 106
- Individual Shepherd's Pies 107
- Sweetcorn Patties 108
- Easy Vegetarian Pizza 109
- Zucchini Risotto 110
- Cauliflower Cheese Fritters 112
- Yummy Fishy Pie 113
- Vegetarian Nuggets 114
- Patty Towers 115
- Easy Peasy Chicken on a Stick 116
- Mixed Grilled Sandwich 117
- Indonesian Style Chicken Skewers 118
- Sticky Chicken 120
- Stir Fry Cauliflower Rice 121
- Tasty Tofu Stir-Fry 122
- Citrus Stir Fry 123
- Zesty Fried Chicken 124
- Spicy Shrimp Wraps 125
- Buttery Tofu 126
- Speedy Stroganoff 128
- Salmon and Noodle Stir Fry 129
- Chicken Soup 130
- Cheesy Chicken Dippers 131
- Sausage Tray Bake 132
- Beef and Linguini Stir-fry 133

DESSERTS 135
- Blueberry Crumble 136
- Syrupy Apples 138
- Summer Lollies 139
- Peach and Blueberry Bake 140
- Refrigerator Cheesecake 141
- Strawberries and Cream Shortcake 142
- Not So Foolish Fool! 144
- Banana Cake Squares 145
- Very Berry Cheesecakes 146
- Nutty Coconut Ice Cream 148
- Aussie Pavlova 149
- Super Fruity Fruit Salad 150
- Cold Fruit Custard 152
- Panna Cotta with Passion 153
- Chocolate Trifle 154
- Raspberry Layer Cake 155
- Speedy Sorbet 156
- Chunky Compote 158
- Brazilian Inspired Mousse 159
- Rich Fruit Loaves 160

Introduction

Parenting takes on a whole new level of difficulty as your child starts to master the art of walking—and running—around and toddling all over the place. Toddlers are very active and require a lot of energy and nutrition to maintain their physical, mental, and emotional health, and develop properly.

This book will make preparing meals more convenient by providing healthy, nutritious recipes that are quick and easy to prepare without the need to go to a specialized store for rare ingredients. This book will also provide you with information about what your child needs to eat and avoid, what nutrition they need daily, and even a few extra tips and tricks.

CHAPTER 1

Benefits of Cooking for Your Toddler

Benefits of Cooking For Your Toddler

You might feel the need to ask why you should bother cooking specifically for your toddler, rather than just letting them eat smaller portions of the meals you cook every day. There is more than one answer to that, and cooking for your toddler holds several benefits.

The first, and most important benefit of centering your meals around your toddler is the nutritional value of the meal. A toddler's body is still in the early development phases, and its chemical composition is different from the body of a fully grown adult or even a slightly older child. Toddlers have very different nutritional needs in order to keep their bodies working properly and developing healthily. Many of the foods adults and older children eat often lack some of the nutrients toddlers need in their daily lives or contain too much of nutrients that can be harmful to your toddler. By cooking meals that cater to your toddler's specific needs, you can ensure that they grow up healthy and strong.

Another important reason why you should cook for your toddler is for the development of good eating habits. The early years are when you can have the largest influence on the eating habits and skills your child will have in the future. By cooking healthy foods for your child, you can teach them to eat healthily and stick to proper portion sizes in the future.

By avoiding processed foods and unnecessary added sugars in their daily meals, your toddler will not develop a taste for them, and will not crave or overindulge in these types of foods when they are older. This can also be a good opportunity to teach your child to eat healthier alternatives to sugary foods, such as fruits and berries instead of candy.

You can also avoid the bane of every parent known as the picky eater. By cooking a wide variety of meals and exposing your child to as many foods as possible, you can teach your toddler not to be too picky and difficult with what they eat.

CHAPTER 2
What Your Toddler Should Be Eating

Everyone has foods they should and should not be eating, especially toddlers and small children. It's very important to provide your child with the right types of food and to avoid any foods that might be unhealthy or even harmful for your toddler. It's also important to manage portion sizes, as too much or too little of any food type can throw your toddler's health and nutrition out of balance.

Foods Your Toddler Should Eat

There is a very wide variety of healthy foods your toddler can enjoy, making it easy to give them something different every day.

Milk

Somewhere between the first 12 to 24 months, you may start thinking about gradually stopping breastfeeding your child. Milk is still an important part of a child's daily diet. Your toddler should drink about 2 - 3 cups of cow's milk every day, and for children younger than 24 months, you should offer them pasteurized whole milk to ensure they get all the nutrients they need. After two years, it is safe to start offering your child milk with a lower fat content, such as skim or 1% milk. After the age of 2, it's also better to limit the times your child drinks milk to their meal times rather than any time throughout the day.

Dairy Products

Other dairy products, such as cheese and yogurt are a good way to make sure your toddler gets enough calcium in their diet even if they're not fond of milk in general. It's best to stick to softer cheeses and products such as cottage cheese rather than harder cheeses that might be difficult for your toddler to chew. Once your toddler is a little older and their teeth have started to come in, you can give them grated or diced cheese that they can chew on their own. It's also better to use full fat yogurt in the early stages of your child's development rather than fat free.

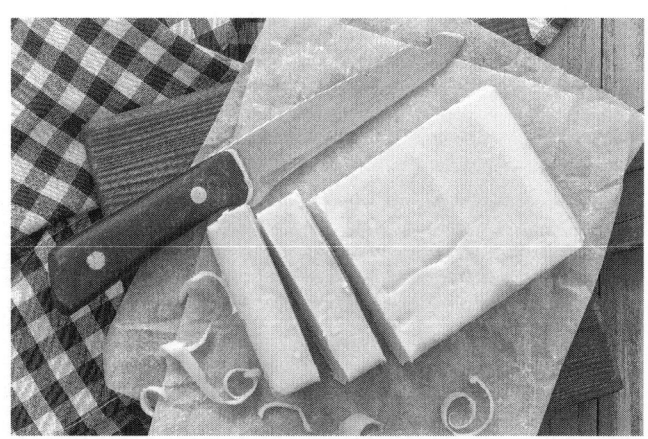

Fruits and Vegetables

Fruits and vegetables are the cornerstone of any healthy diet and are especially important for toddlers. This is where they will get most of the vitamins and minerals they need to develop and grow, as well as boost their immune system. It's always better to give your toddler softer fruits such as bananas, papaya, watermelon, apricots, and peaches. It's important to stay with fresh or frozen fruits as much as possible for the healthiest option, and fruit should be sliced into small pieces that are easy to eat. Older toddlers can also eat dried fruit that has been soaked until soft. Apples are incredibly difficult for toddlers to eat, but can be mashed and cooked into a puree for them.

Vegetables should always be cooked well until they are soft enough for your toddler to eat without effort. For smaller toddlers under two years old, it's best to stick to simple vegetables like cauliflower, broccoli, pumpkin, potatoes, and carrots. Vegetables like peas and corn should wait until a little later since they can be a choking hazard for very small children.

You should try to encourage your child to eat a cup of fruits and a cup of vegetables each day.

Whole Grains

Your child needs a good amount of grains in their diet to provide energy, fiber, and many other trace elements of important nutrients. Whole grains are much better for your child than processed grains, as they retain all their nutrients and minerals. It's also a very healthy eating habit to teach your child for the future. The best ways to give your child whole grains is through whole wheat bread, whole grain rice and pasta, and cereals made from oats, barley, and wheat. It's also a good idea to look for iron-fortified cereals, as these will help ensure your child gets enough iron in their diet. Ideally, your child should eat roughly three ounces of grains daily. When giving your child whole grain foods, it's important to cook your rice and pasta well and thoroughly soak their cold cereal in milk or water to make sure everything is soft enough. While it's a great idea to make a simple sauce to serve together with your rice or pasta, you should wait until

your toddler has passed two years of age before starting to serve combined dishes like casseroles or macaroni and cheese.

Proteins

Even at this young age, proteins are very important for your child, and luckily there are many different sources for you to choose from. Most types of meat, such as beef, pork, poultry, and fish are safe to serve to your toddler as long as you make sure to cook them properly and cut them into small pieces. It's better if you stick to your leaner meat and softer cuts to make the meat easy for your child to eat. When preparing poultry and fish, it is vital to make sure that they are completely boneless.

Eggs, beans, and tofu are also a great source of protein for your toddler, and even a thin layer of peanut butter spread onto a slice of bread can do the job.

A toddler should eat about two ounces of protein every day.

Honey

While it should be limited to small amounts, your child does need some sugar in their diet, and honey—especially raw honey—is a much healthier and more natural option than refined, processed sugars. Of course, you shouldn't just give your child a bowl of honey and try to deal with the mess afterward; you can drizzle a little honey over your toddler's cereal or carrots to make the dish a little sweeter. It's important to use honey in moderation in order to make sure your toddler doesn't get used to sweet foods.

Foods Your Toddler Should Avoid

There are, unfortunately, a fair amount of foods you should avoid giving to your toddler, some for more obvious reasons than others.

Processed Foods

Most foods, especially grains, tend to lose most of their nutritional value when they are processed, which means that your child will not get all the nutrients they need. Your child will also eat more processed foods than whole foods before they feel full, which will result in your child learning the bad habit of eating a lot of food at once, likely leading to overeating in the future. Many processed foods also contain more calories, carbs, and other added chemicals that can be harmful for your child.

Added Sugar

Added sugar is another health hazard that can turn into a bad eating habit. Too much sugar, especially refined sugar, can lead to heart disease, high cholesterol, and diabetes. Because of this, you should avoid foods that contain added sugar, such as candy, chocolate, soda, and several types of fruit juice. It's much better to let your child take in their daily sugar through fruit and small amounts of honey. Foods containing a large amount of sugar will also lead to tooth decay.

Small, Round Foods

It's surprising how easy it is for food to become a choking hazard, especially for toddlers. At this young age children are still earning to chew and don't know how to do it properly yet. Especially foods with a round shape, like cherry tomatoes, grapes, hard candies, popcorn, cough drops, etc. are hard to keep in place while chewing, and can slip into the throat very easily. Many of these kinds of foods should be avoided, and grapes and cherry tomatoes should be cut into quarters before giving them to your toddler. Nuts and seeds also fall into this category. If you want to expose your child to nuts, you should nut butters and spreads. You should also avoid foods like cherries and olives that haven't been pitted.

Large Pieces of Food

This is another choking hazard, as it is very likely that your toddler will chew only a little bit or not at all before

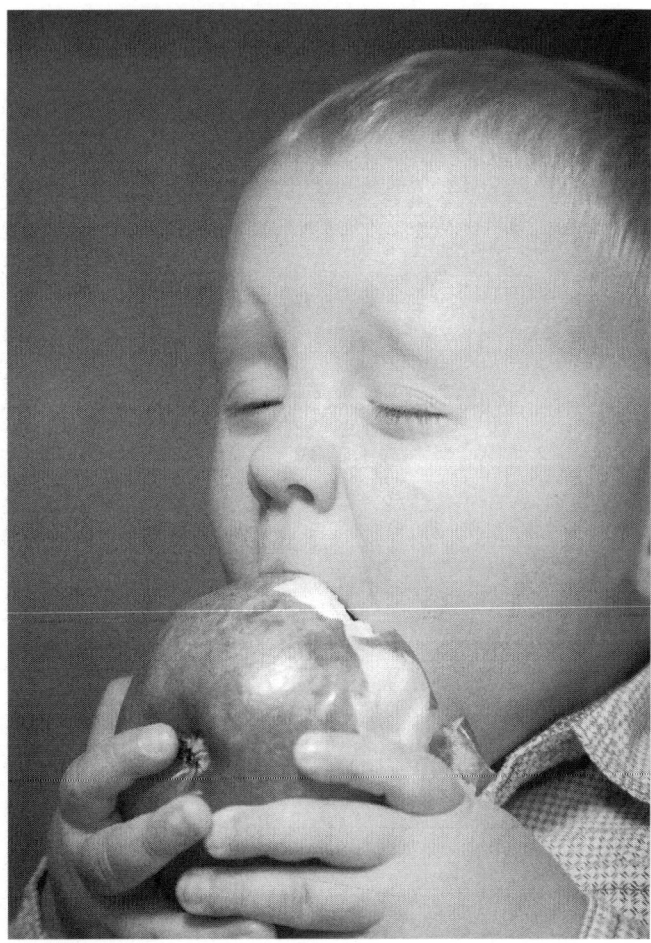

susceptible to any food-borne illnesses. Food that hasn't been fully cooked often carries germs that your toddler's body simply cannot guard against. The same rule applies to eggs, and you should avoid a runny yolk and any products that contain raw egg. Raw or undercooked vegetables are also fairly hard and difficult for your child to chew, making this a choking hazard as well.

Raw milk that hasn't been pasteurized is also a food you shouldn't give your toddler in order to protect them from food-borne illnesses and food poisoning.

Sticky Foods

Very sticky foods are another health hazard, as small pieces can get stuck in your child's throat. Marshmallows are especially high-risk since they are also soft, making it easy to accidentally swallow pieces that would normally be too large. The same happens with large blobs of peanut butter, and rather than giving your child a spoon with a chunk of peanut butter, you should spread it onto pieces of toast or crackers in a thin layer.

Allergens

Children can start manifesting allergic reactions to specific food types from a very young age. You should always keep a close eye on your toddler while they are eating, and you should be vigilant for any signs of an allergic reaction. If you do suspect that your child has an allergy, you should consult your pediatrician immediately.

While many children can grow out of their allergies later in life, it can still be difficult dealing with these allergens, especially when it comes to toddlers who don't understand that the food they might love very much can be the source of a lot of their pain and suffering and can hold risks for them.

The best way to deal with food allergies is to find a similar, child-safe replacement ingredient for an allergen, rather than simply trying to just cut it out of your child's diet. We'll be taking a closer, more detailed look at specific allergens and their replacements a little later in this book.

swallowing, and the large pieces will block your child's airway. Always make sure that you cut any food your toddler eats into small pieces, even if the food is fairly soft. Hot dogs and sausage links are especially risky, since simply cutting them into small rounds increases the risk of choking. If you want to give your child a hotdog, you should cut it lengthwise first, and then cut it into smaller pieces.

Tender Meat & Raw Vegetables

Your toddler's body hasn't had nearly as much time to develop a proper immune system, and they can be very

CHAPTER 3
Make Food for The Whole Family

Many first-time parents believe that it might become necessary to cook separate meals for their toddler and the rest of the family, but just because your toddler can't eat everything you can, doesn't mean you can't eat everything your toddler can. The foods that are healthy for small children are also very healthy for older children, teens, adults, and even the elderly. It can be very easy to adapt a single meal or recipe to suit the needs of the whole family—even the youngest—without a large amount of extra time and effort.

The first step in cooking for both your toddler and the rest of the family is to find ingredients everybody likes. While everyone has foods they like and dislike, there is bound to be some common ground with basic ingredients everybody is happy with. Cooking meals and finding recipes that combine everyone's favorite will make mealtimes a pleasure for the whole family. You can also remove or replace a few ingredients in some of your best recipes with something more child-friendly, like mixing peanut butter into a dish requiring nuts, or preparing the ingredients in a more child-friendly manner. In many cases, you can prepare a completely toddler-friendly meal, separate their portion from the main dish, and then simply add a few extra ingredients your family wants for the last few minutes of cooking. Cooking for the whole family with a toddler in the house is a simple matter of everyone meeting each other in the middle.

Another aspect of making meals more suitable for the whole family is taking a look at the state of the ingredients. The basic taste of an ingredient isn't the only factor that can influence whether someone likes it or not. In many cases, especially with toddlers, color and texture can determine whether your child will eat their food. A toddler will feel less inclined to eat a food if the color looks a little odd or unappealing, and the same applies to the texture. Fresh ingredients are also more likely to appeal to both your toddler and the rest of your family than something that might have been canned or frozen. Simply by paying attention to something as small as this, you can improve your chances of the entire family enjoying the meal. The condition of the ingredients also refers to how they are prepared and cooked. How long you cook any ingredient not only determines the texture, but can also have a large influence on the taste. It often happens that family members prefer their meat a little more tender, their veggies a little more raw so that they're still crispy, or even prefer some ingredients completely raw. Toddlers, on the other hand, need to have their ingredients thoroughly cooked, both to ensure their health and to make their food easy and comfortable to eat. This can often cause a problem when cooking for the whole family, but you can easily cook the family's meal together and separate a portion for your toddler to cook just a little bit longer at the end. You can also start cooking your toddler's a little sooner than the rest of the meal.

Another simple way to cater to your toddler in the family meal is simply to cut the ingredients a little smaller. By cutting the ingredients in a meal to the size appropriate for a toddler rather than how you've always cut them, most recipes instantly become a lot more toddler-friendly with minimal effort.

Special Diets

Something many parents struggle with is whether a special diet or dietary lifestyle the family follows is safe for their toddlers or not. There are many diets that cut out specific types of ingredients, and some are definitely more suitable for toddlers than others.

Vegetarian and Vegan Diet

These are two of the most common diets that can raise the question of suitability, but as long as you put in a little effort, a vegetarian or vegan diet won't cause any problems. There are many toddler-friendly alternatives that are great sources of iron, protein, and calcium, such as beans, spinach, soy milk, and tofu. It will require careful planning, and you'll have to keep a close eye on the nutrients your child gets on a daily basis, but your toddler doesn't need meat and other animal products to stay healthy.

Gluten-Free

While a gluten-free diet can hold health benefits for adults, this diet is not safe for toddlers. Products that contain gluten also contain your child's main source of carbs, as well as several other nutrients your child cannot go without. A gluten-free diet also contains a large amount of rice, which tends to absorb traces of arsenic from the ground. While a small amount of rice every now and then is fine, too much rice can damage your child's health. You should only switch to a gluten-free diet if your child is allergic to gluten.

23

CHAPTER 4
Getting the Right Nutrition

If you are reading this, chances are your baby has started showing signs that they are ready for solids. Starting solid foods is quite exciting and is a significant milestone in your baby's, life. It can be slightly messy, so prepare yourself for it. Chances are you're feeling a little overwhelmed and nervous at this point. You don't have to worry because this can be quite fun. Once you are equipped with the right tools and recipes, making baby food at home is incredibly simple. But before you start making baby food, you need to understand the basics involved.

Getting enough nutrition for your toddler is extremely important, but you should also take care that you maintain the right balance as well. Here is a simple chart to help you plan your daily meals accordingly:

Food Group	Servings Per Day	Examples of Single Serving
Grains & Wheat	6	1-2 Crackers 1/4 slice bread, 1/4 cup cereal, rice, pasta
Fruits	1/2 piece of fruit	1/4 cup juice
Vegetables	2 - 3	Add more as your child grows older
Proteins	2	1 oz cooked meat, 1/2 eggs, 1tbsp peanut butter on bread
Dairy	2 - 3	1/2 cup milk, 1/3 cup yogurt

One of the best ways to ensure maximum nutrition is to buy seasonal produce. The main reason why people buy seasonal produce is because it's cheaper, but produce that is in season is also much fresher and much more nutritious than fruits and vegetables that have been imported, canned, or frozen. It can, however, be a little tricky to be certain which fruit and vegetables are in season and which aren't, but here is a simple table to help guide you in the right direction:

Spring

Seasonal fruits: Lemons, oranges, strawberries, avocados.

Seasonal vegetables: Peas, mushrooms, lettuce, leeks, cauliflower, carrots, cabbage, broccoli

Summer

Seasonal fruits: Lemons, oranges, peaches, raspberries, strawberries, avocados

Seasonal vegetables: Tomatoes, lettuce, green beans, corn, cucumber, carrots, cabbage

Fall

Seasonal fruits: Grapes, lemons, peaches, pears, raspberries, strawberries, apples, avocados

Seasonal vegetables: Tomatoes, sweet potatoes, pumpkins, mushrooms, lettuce, cucumber, cauliflower, carrots, cabbage, broccoli, spinach

Winter

Seasonal fruits: Lemons, oranges, avocados

Seasonal vegetables: Mushrooms, leeks, kale, cauliflower, carrots, cabbage, broccoli

Another element that can throw your toddler's nutrition out of balance is an allergy. Many of the foods children are commonly allergic to contain vital nutrients, and it is important to find a suitable replacement to help keep your child healthy. Here are some of the most common food allergies children suffer from and their replacements:

Allergens and their replacements

Milk: Soy, coconut, almond, or rice milk

Eggs: Chia seeds, flaxseed, other protein sources

Fish & Shellfish: Lean proteins, mushrooms

Peanuts & tree nuts: Seed butter, chickpeas, other protein sources.

Wheat: Rye, spelt

What About the Rest of the Family?

Even if you are focusing on your toddler, you shouldn't neglect the nutrition of the rest of your family. Every age group requires a different balance of nutrients and calories they take in every day. While it is true that those who are more active require more calories, there is still a basic guide to how much everyone needs every day.

- Children from 2-3 years need 1,000-1,400 calories
- Children between the ages of 4 and 8 need 1,400-1,600 calories
- Children from 9-13 need 1,600 to 2,000 calories
- Teens between 14 and 18 need 2,000 calories
- Adults from 19-30 need 2,00-2,200 calories
- Adults from 30-50 need 2,000 calories
- Adults older than 50 need 1,800 calories

The list above is a general average, and each family might require more or less calories depending on how active their daily routine is.

As you grow, the daily portions you need are similar to the first chart provided, but the portions become bigger. The best way to measure the ideal portion size is to use your hand. Anything that fits comfortably in the palm of your hand is a single portion for you.

Something else to take into consideration is to keep your gut microbiome healthy, which will improve your and your family's overall health a great deal. Foods that are great for feeding the microbiome are grass-fed meats, fruits and vegetables with little to no starch, nut and seed butters, lentils, fermented vegetables, herbs, and spices.

Dealing With Leftovers

Leftovers are a natural result of almost any meal, including your toddler's. Almost all types of food can last up to three days in the fridge before they start losing their nutritional value and can be kept for even longer when properly frozen or vacuum sealed. If you want to refrigerate or freeze food, it's important to let it cool down first. Once your food has reached room temperature, place it in the refrigerator, even if you want to freeze it. Once the food is cold, you can transfer it to freezer bags. It's important to use proper freezer bags that will keep your food fresher than container bags and to remove as much air as possible, which will help protect your food from freezer burn and preserve the quality of the food. You should also store your food in small portions, sticking to thin layers. This will make sure your food freezes and thaws quickly, reducing the possibility of bacteria in your food. Once your freezer bags are properly sealed, spread them evenly throughout your freezer to let everything freeze as quickly and evenly as possible to preserve nutrition.

When thawing your food, you should plan ahead and let your food thaw in the refrigerator and not at room temperature. Once your frozen food is completely thawed, you can reheat it immediately or keep it in the fridge for a day or two. If you're thawing food in the microwave, you will have to reheat it immediately.

When reheating food, exposure to liquids like water and oil and high temperatures results in nutrient loss. This means that the best way to reheat your leftovers is to use the microwave, which is the quickest and doesn't need extra liquids. You should always make sure your food is always covered with a damp paper towel to ensure it doesn't dry out and lose nutrients that way.

Investing in a vacuum sealer is also a great way to preserve nutrition, as the low exposure to oxygen will maintain the nutrients in your food and prevent the growth of mold and bacteria. Vacuum sealing your food before freezing is also the best way to keep your frozen foods as nutritious as possible.

CHAPTER 5
Solving a Few Problems

Two of the biggest problems all parents of toddlers have to deal with are picky eaters and children who don't want to eat new foods. These problems often walk hand in hand and can sometimes be handled simultaneously. There are a few simple, easy, ways to encourage your child to eat different, new foods.

Let your toddler help cooking: By letting your child do small, simple tasks to help you while you're preparing your food, they will be much more invested in the meal, and will be more likely to eat new foods or foods they don't like simply because they were part of the process.

Mix in some favorites: This works great for both picky eaters and new foods. When you serve new or unfavorable food together with your toddler's favorites, they will be more comfortable with these foods. These favorites will also help hide or improve the taste of the food your toddler doesn't usually like.

Don't compromise or bargain: When a picky toddler sticks to a single dish and refuses to eat something else, you shouldn't make that dish every day to please them. You are in charge of your child's meals, and it is your choice what to give them. Even if your child refuses to eat what you put in front of them, don't give in and give them something else; toddlers are smart enough not to starve out of spite.

Eat with your child: Toddlers tend to follow your example, and if you show them that you're eating and enjoying a new or disliked food, they will feel safer and be more inclined to try the food out.

Provide options: Toddlers try to show some independence by choosing their food, and you want to support that. Rather than asking your child what they want to eat at the risk of getting the same answer for every meal, give them a few meal options that they can choose from.

Be patient and persistent: Your toddler won't learn to eat new food overnight. When trying to encourage your child to eat new food, start out with small portions and be prepared to fail the first few times. Your child won't instantly like the new food, and you will have to give them this new food several times before they feel comfortable with it.

Sometimes your toddler may not be the only picky eater in the house, and the whole family can have trouble agreeing on meals. If this happens, it's important to

establish a hierarchy in the kitchen and determine who has the final say when it comes to meals (this would usually be the person cooking most of the meals). Then it's time to put down some ground rules on what foods and meal types will and will not be allowed. This way, everyone will not always be 100% happy, but they won't be forced to eat something they absolutely hate. If you're still having trouble getting the family to agree on meals, let everyone take turns choosing meals.

One of the big reasons why your toddler may not be eating the way they should can be that their food simply isn't appealing to them. Toddlers get bored easily, and you should try to make mealtimes as fun as playtime by making their food more fun and interesting. One of the most effective ways to do this is to give your toddler lots of finger foods that they can dip in sauces and don't need to struggle with a spoon to eat. Another way is to make sure you use foods that are bright and colorful, and use a good variety of colors to draw their attention. You can also incorporate your toddler's current interests, like a love for stars or their favorite cartoons, and find ways to incorporate those into their meals. Lastly, you can play around a little with the way you present your toddler's food. Cut the food into interesting shapes, arrange different food items into a simple image on the plate, like a smiley face or a rainbow, or make mini foods that are simply smaller than they normally are.

One of the most useful tools a parent can keep in mind when cooking for their toddler is the use of 'umami'. Umami sounds like an exotic term but it is really just the concept of intense flavor, somewhere between sweet, salty, bitter and sour. It adds surprise and richness to food, and excites the tongue. Some people define umami as the use of 'msg'(monosodium glutamate), however this is not recommended! Healthy umami can be included in your toddler's foods through the addition of small amounts of the following natural ingredients, sprinkled on top off foods or added to sauces and soups: dried and ground mushrooms; soy sauce or tamari; miso paste; oyster sauce; tomato sauce or paste; sun-dried tomatoes; seaweed (dried or pickled); pickled vegetables; anchovies (small amounts); aged cheeses and cheese rinds; kimchi; bacon. Just add tiny amounts to foods your toddler may not be too excited about, or to give a flavorful change of pace when serving simple standards like steamed carrots. You and your toddler will discover what umami flavors they most enjoy through trial and error, and these may change as well with time. Consider umami your friend in the kitchen, able to come to the rescue when nothing seems to be satisfying your toddler or when adored foods become boring.

CHAPTER 6

Breakfast For The Whole Family

Tasty Breakfast Salad

A delicious and nutritious way to start the day. Use any or all of the ingredients listed or just use up what you have in the fridge!

Servings: 4 Portions   Prep Time: 15 Mins   Cook Time: 10 Mins

Ingredients

4 eggs, hard or soft boiled

8 slices bacon

1 head of lettuce, washed and leaves separated

1 avocado

2 large tomatoes, sliced

1 red or yellow pepper, sliced

50g cheese, any variety will do

OPTIONAL:

Broccoli

Mushrooms

Zucchini

Diced ham

Roasted sweet potatoes

Roasted potatoes

HERBS:

Cilantro, basil, parsley, etc.

Directions

1. Boil the eggs in a pan of simmering water and cook for 6 minutes or a little longer depending on how you like them.
2. Fry the bacon till crispy, then place on a paper towel to remove the excess fat.
3. Wash and prepare all the vegetables.
4. Start to build the salad on individual plates. Divide the lettuce leaves between the plates.
5. Add the slices of avocado, tomato, peppers and any other veg that you are using.
6. Top with the bacon and then remove the shell from the boiled egg, cut in half and place in the center.
7. Grate the cheese over the top.

NUTRITIONAL INFO: CALORIES: 349 | SODIUM: 153MG | DIETARY FIBER: 7.8G
TOTAL FAT: 23.2G | TOTAL CARBS: 19.1G | PROTEIN: 18.7G.

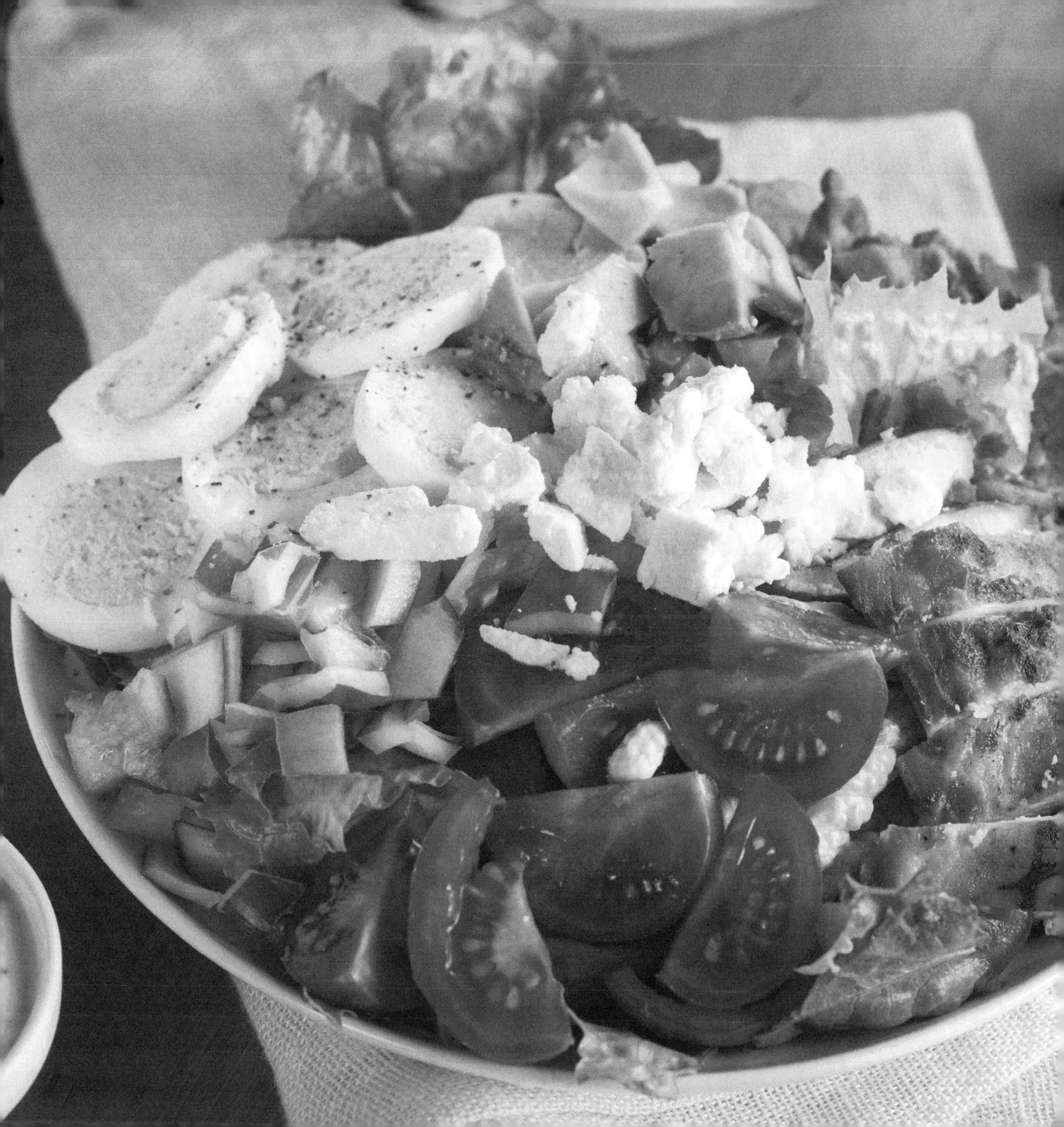

Breakfast Casserole

This dish takes a little more time to prepare, so it's perfect for a relaxed weekend brunch. Serve with a salad or with freshly diced avocados on top.

Servings: 6 Portions   **Prep Time: 15 Minutes**   **Cook Time: 45 Minutes**

Ingredients

- 6 - 8 slices turkey bacon
- 1 can crescent roll dough
- 1 bag frozen shredded hash browns
- 12 eggs
- Veggies of your choice (spinach, mushrooms, zucchini, broccoli, etc.)
- Salt and pepper to taste
- Grated cheddar cheese

Directions

1. Preheat the oven to 350°F.
2. Fry the bacon, once done set aside to cool.
3. Grease a baking dish with non-stick olive oil spray, place the crescent roll dough evenly on the bottom of the baking dish.
4. Take the frozen shredded hash browns and place evenly on top of the crescent roll dough.
5. Beat the eggs together in a bowl. Add your veggies then season with salt and pepper.
6. Pour the egg mixture evenly on top of shredded hash browns
7. Place in the oven and cook for 45 minutes, the egg should be cooked through.
8. Remove from the oven and grate the cheese evenly across the top.
9. Place back in the oven until the cheese has melted and the casserole is bubbling.

NUTRITIONAL INFO: CALORIES: 295 | SODIUM: 137MG | DIETARY FIBER: 1G
TOTAL FAT: 18.7G | TOTAL CARBS: 12.9G | PROTEIN: 19.9G.

Vegetarian Breakfast Tostadas

These Mexican inspired tostadas are a great weekend breakfast option! Not only do they look awesome, but they're easy to make and taste super fresh.

Servings: 8 Tostadas **Prep Time: 30 Minutes** **Cook Time: 10 Minutes**

Ingredients

8 (100% corn) tortillas

1 tablespoon olive oil

2 cups refried beans, warmed through

8 eggs, fried or scrambled

1/2 cup grated cheddar cheese

2 cups pico de gallo

Optional garnishes, for serving:

Your favorite hot sauce or salsa, avocado, and/or crumbled Cotija or feta cheese

Directions

1. Preheat the oven to 400°F, line two large baking sheets with parchment paper.

2. Brush both sides of each tortilla lightly with olive oil. Arrange 4 tortillas across each baking sheet. Bake for 10 to 12 minutes, turning halfway, until each tortilla is golden and lightly crisp. Set aside.

3. Meanwhile, warm the refried beans and cook the eggs to your liking.

4. To assemble, spread the beans over each tortilla. Top with a sprinkle of cheese, cooked egg, then top with Pico de Gallo. Add any of the optional garnishes of your choice.

NUTRITIONAL INFO: CALORIES: 263 | SODIUM: 457MG | DIETARY FIBER: 4.9G
TOTAL FAT: 11.3G | TOTAL CARBS: 28.9G | PROTEIN: 10.4G.

Broccoli and Cheese Mini Quiches

Packed with veggies and cheesy goodness, these little quiches can be prepared the day before making them an easy and healthy way to start your day.

Servings: 6 Portions   **Prep Time: 10 Minutes**   **Cook Time: 20 Minutes**

Ingredients

3 large eggs
1 (12 oz) can evaporated milk
6 ounces broccoli, chopped and steamed
1 cup cheddar cheese, finely grated
1/2 teaspoon lemon pepper seasoning
4 mini sweet peppers, sliced into 6 rings each

Directions

1. Preheat the oven to 350°F. Lightly grease a nonstick 12-cup muffin pan.
2. Gently beat the eggs in a medium sized bowl. Add the evaporated milk, broccoli, grated cheese and lemon pepper seasoning. Mix well.
3. Divide the mixture evenly between muffin cups. Top each one with 2 pepper rings.
4. Bake in the oven for 20 - 25 minutes, or until a knife inserted in the center comes out clean. Allow to cool in the pan for 15 minutes. Run a knife around the sides to loosen and remove from the pan.
5. Serve immediately or refrigerate up to 3 days.

NUTRITIONAL INFO: CALORIES: 223 | SODIUM: 223MG | DIETARY FIBER: 1.9G
TOTAL FAT: 13.3G | TOTAL CARBS: 14.1G | PROTEIN: 13.3G.

Veggie Frittata

Packed with veggies and flavor, this one pan frittata is not only delicious for breakfast but can be enjoyed at any time of the day.

Servings: 6 Portions   Prep Time: 10 Minutes   Cook Time: 20 Minutes

Ingredients

6 eggs
2 tablespoons whole milk or single cream
35g (1/2 cup) cheddar cheese, grated
1 teaspoon dried oregano
1/2 teaspoon pepper
Salt (to taste)
1 tablespoon olive oil
1 onion, finely chopped
1 teaspoon garlic, crushed
1 red bell pepper (capsicum), finely chopped
1 carrot, grated
190g broccolini or broccoli
150g (1 cup) peas

Directions

1. Preheat oven to 425°F.
2. In a mixing bowl, whisk the eggs, milk or cream, cheese, herbs and seasoning till well combined.
3. Heat oil in an oven proof frying pan, add the onion and garlic and cook for approximately 5 mins.
4. Add the bell pepper (capsicum) and carrot and cook for a further two minutes.
5. Add the broccolini and cook for another 2 mins. Stir in the peas.
6. Pour the egg mixture over the vegetables. Stir to distribute the mixture evenly across the pan.
7. Cook on the stove top until the edge of the frittata has turned lighter in color, this should take a few minutes.
8. Transfer the pan to the oven and bake for 10 mins. Take the frittata out of the oven when the middle still has a slight jiggle to it or when it is just set.
9. Cool in the pan for 5 mins, slice and serve.

NUTRITIONAL INFO: CALORIES: 162 | SODIUM: 120MG | DIETARY FIBER: 3.2G
TOTAL FAT: 9.1G | TOTAL CARBS: 11G | PROTEIN: 10G.

Weekday Breakfast Burritos

These burritos are perfect for a busy weekday morning, quick to make and super tasty to eat!

Servings: 8 Burritos   Prep Time: 5 Mins   Cook Time: 15 Mins

Ingredients

6 eggs
1/2 cup milk
1 cup cheddar cheese, grated
1/2 teaspoon salt
1/2 teaspoon black pepper
8 (8-inch) flour tortillas

Directions

1. In a mixing bowl whisk the eggs and milk.
2. Pour into a large nonstick pan and scramble over a medium heat.
3. Once the eggs are cooked, allow them to cool then add the grated cheese, salt and pepper.
4. Fill each tortilla with some of the egg mixture and roll up.

NUTRITIONAL INFO: CALORIES: 252 | SODIUM: 688MG | DIETARY FIBER: 1G
TOTAL FAT: 11.3G | TOTAL CARBS: 25.3G | PROTEIN: 12.2G.

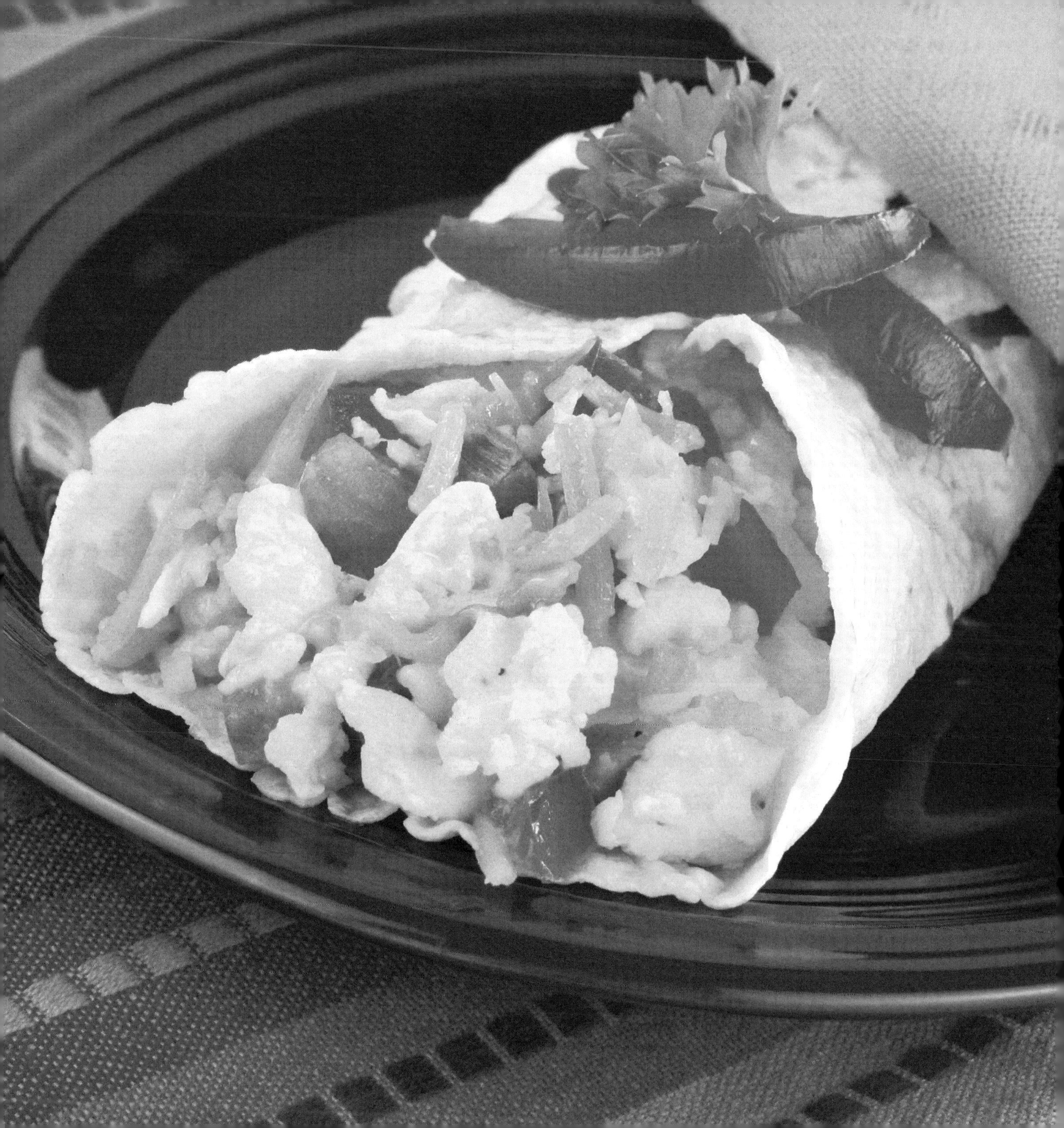

Roasted Veggie Hash

Roasting brings out the best flavor in vegetables, so even the pickiest of small people won't be able to resist this delicious winter hash!

Servings: 4   Prep Time: 15 Minutes   Cook Time: 40 Minutes

Ingredients

300g sweet potato (cut into cubes)

1/2 cauliflower (cut into florets)

1 zucchini (thinly sliced)

250g potato (cut into cubes)

1 onion (cut into wedges)

400g pumpkin (peeled and cut into pieces)

1 teaspoon fresh rosemary (finely chopped)

1 tablespoon olive oil

1 cup organic chicken stock

1/4 cup parmesan cheese (grated)

1/4 cup cheddar cheese (grated)

Directions

1. Preheat oven to 430°F.
2. Put all the vegetables along with the rosemary and olive oil in a large deep oven tray. Season with salt and pepper, then toss to ensure the veggies are evenly coated.
3. Pour the chicken stock over the vegetables. Roast for 15 minutes. Toss the vegetables in the tray again and roast for another 15 minutes or until tender.
4. Using a fork, roughly mash vegetables and work into a rectangle shape. Sprinkle with both the cheeses.
5. Roast for 10 more minutes or until golden and crisp.

NUTRITIONAL INFO: CALORIES: 279 | SODIUM: 342MG | DIETARY FIBER: 7G
TOTAL FAT: 7.5G | TOTAL CARBS: 48.6G | PROTEIN: 8.8G.

Strawberry and Hidden Veg Smoothie

Delicious, nutritious and quick to make. If you prefer you can always substitute soy or oat milk to make a dairy-free smoothie instead.

Servings: 2   Prep Time: 5 Minutes   Cook Time: No cooking

Ingredients

BASE:

1 cup strawberries (fresh or frozen)

1 banana, sliced and frozen

1/2 cup fresh or frozen raw cauliflower florets

1 cup milk

Maple syrup or honey to taste

Try adding in one of two of the ingredients below to the base recipe to make your own special smoothie:

1/2 cup baby spinach

1 tablespoon shredded unsweetened coconut

1/2 cup frozen mango

2 tablespoons rolled oats.

2 tablespoons cashews

1 - 2 tablespoons peanut butter (or almond butter)

1/2 cup baby spinach

Directions

1. Put all the ingredients into a blender.
2. Blend the ingredients for at least 30 seconds or until very smooth.
3. Serve immediately.

NUTRITIONAL INFO: CALORIES: 220 | SODIUM: 75MG | DIETARY FIBER: 4G
TOTAL FAT: 7G | TOTAL CARBS: 36.1G | PROTEIN: 7.2G.

Spinach and Banana Blender Muffins

Moist, yummy and made in the blender quick as a flash. These muffins store well, so you can make them ahead of time and just pull them out of the fridge to serve.

Servings: 12 Muffins   **Prep Time: 10 Minutes**   **Cook Time: 18 - 20 Minutes**

Ingredients

1 large ripe banana, sliced

2 cups lightly packed baby spinach

3/4 cups milk

1/4 cup honey

2 tablespoons butter, melted and cooled

2 eggs

1 teaspoon vanilla extract

1 cup rolled oats

1 teaspoon baking soda

1/8 teaspoon salt

1 cup whole-wheat flour (or gluten-free flour blend)

Mini chocolate chips, optional

Directions

1. Preheat the oven to 375 °F. Grease a 12-hole muffin tin with nonstick spray.
2. Put all of the ingredients, except the flour and chocolate chips into a blender.
3. Blend until smooth, stopping to scrape down the sides as needed. The mixture should resemble a smoothie.
4. Next, pulse in the flour to combine, or stir it in gently.
5. Pour the batter into the muffin tin, filling each case until 3/4 full. If you are using chocolate chips, evenly sprinkle over the top.
6. Bake for 18 - 20 minutes or until firm to the touch. The muffins should be lightly browned around the edges.
7. Remove from the oven, use a paring knife to loosen the edges from the tins, then transfer to a wire rack to cool.
8. Serve slightly warm, at room temperature, or chilled.

NUTRITIONAL INFO: CALORIES: 133 | SODIUM: 50MG | DIETARY FIBER: 1.4G
TOTAL FAT: 3.6G | TOTAL CARBS: 22G | PROTEIN: 3.7G.

Peanut Butter and Banana Wraps

Nutty, wholesome and filling - a great breakfast that will keep little ones going until lunchtime!

Servings: 2   Prep Time: 10 Minutes   Cook Time: No cooking

Ingredients

2 (8 inch) whole wheat flour tortillas
1/4 cup creamy peanut butter
1/4 cup granola
2 tablespoons honey
2 bananas

Directions

1. Lay out the tortillas, spread peanut butter over each.
2. Sprinkle with granola then drizzle honey on top.
3. Place a banana in the center of each tortilla.
4. Fold in opposite sides; roll up burrito-style.
5. To serve, cut in half.

NUTRITIONAL INFO: CALORIES: 419 | SODIUM: 150MG | DIETARY FIBER: 9.8G
TOTAL FAT: 3.6G | TOTAL CARBS: 18.4G | PROTEIN: 12.3G.

Zucchini Oatmeal Balls

With no baking required, these little energizing Zucchini Oatmeal Balls are full of flavor and nutrients. Have them ready prepared in the refrigerator, making them the perfect grab and go breakfast item.

Servings: 16   **Prep Time: 15 minutes + 1 hour refrigeration time**   **Cook Time: No cooking**

Ingredients

- 1/3 cup coconut oil
- 1/3 cup honey
- 1/2 teaspoon vanilla extract
- 3 cups rolled oats
- 1 teaspoon cinnamon
- 1/2 teaspoon ground nutmeg
- 1/4 cup flax seeds
- 1 cup zucchini, finely grated and patted dry

Directions

1. Melt the coconut oil together with the honey in the microwave for approximately 15 seconds. Mix in the vanilla extract.
2. Next, in a large bowl, put the oats, cinnamon, nutmeg, and flax seeds.
3. Pour over the melted oil and honey mixture. Mix well until everything is properly coated.
4. Add in the zucchini and stir carefully. Then place in the refrigerator.
5. After 30 to 40 minutes remove from the refrigerator and stir the mixture well to ensure everything is well coated in the oil and honey mixture.
6. Using a cookie or ice cream scoop, scoop balls of the oat mixture then press firmly in your hands, so the mixture sticks together. Place the balls on a tray.
7. Finally, place the tray back into the refrigerator to set.

NUTRITIONAL INFO: CALORIES: 130 | SODIUM: 2MG | DIETARY FIBER: 17.1G
TOTAL FAT: 6.1G | TOTAL CARBS: 17.1G | PROTEIN: 2.5G.

Strawberry Quinoa Breakfast Bowl

A healthy and easy to make breakfast bowl. The homemade strawberry milk, fresh berries and almonds are a sure way to bring summer into your home no matter what the weather outside!

Servings: 2   Prep Time: 5 Minutes   Cook Time: No cooking

Ingredients

FOR THE STRAWBERRY MILK:

1/4 cup hemp seeds

3/4 cups water

1 cup strawberries (fresh or frozen)

1 tablespoon maple syrup

2 cups quinoa, cooked

4 strawberries

1/4 cup blueberries

2 tablespoons sliced almonds

Directions

1. Put hemp seeds, water, strawberries and maple syrup into a blender. Blend until smooth and creamy. Set aside.
2. Place the cooked quinoa in a bowl, pour the strawberry milk over and sprinkle on the berries and almonds.
3. Enjoy immediately!

NUTRITIONAL INFO: CALORIES: 341 | SODIUM: 19MG | DIETARY FIBER: 7.8G
TOTAL FAT: 8.8G | TOTAL CARBS: 56.3G | PROTEIN: 11.6G.

Zucchini Pancakes

A yummy breakfast that the whole family will love! Serve them plain or with syrup, jam or even peanut butter.

Servings: 4   Prep Time: 15 Minutes   Cook Time: 15 Minutes

Ingredients

1 cup zucchini, grated and squeezed very dry

2 eggs

1 cup milk

2 tablespoons melted butter, cooled, plus more for cooking

1 teaspoon vanilla extract

1 cup whole wheat flour

1 1/2 teaspoons baking powder

1 teaspoon cinnamon

TOPPINGS:

Maple syrup, apple sauce, peanut butter, or topping of your choice (optional)

Directions

1. In a medium sized bowl, stir together the grated zucchini, eggs, milk, melted butter and vanilla extract.
2. Gently fold in the flour, baking powder, and cinnamon.
3. Heat a nonstick or cast-iron frying pan over medium heat. Add 1 teaspoon butter - stir to melt and coat the surface.
4. To make each pancake, place 1/4 batter in the pan, allow the batter to spread out a little.
5. Cook for 3 - 4 minutes or until you see little bubbles on the surface and that the edges are set. Gently flip over and cook for an additional 3 - 4 minutes.
6. Repeat to make the rest of the batch and serve warm with the topping of your choice.

NUTRITIONAL INFO: CALORIES: 237 | SODIUM: 106MG | DIETARY FIBER: 1.5G
TOTAL FAT: 9.6G | TOTAL CARBS: 29.5G | PROTEIN: 8.4G.

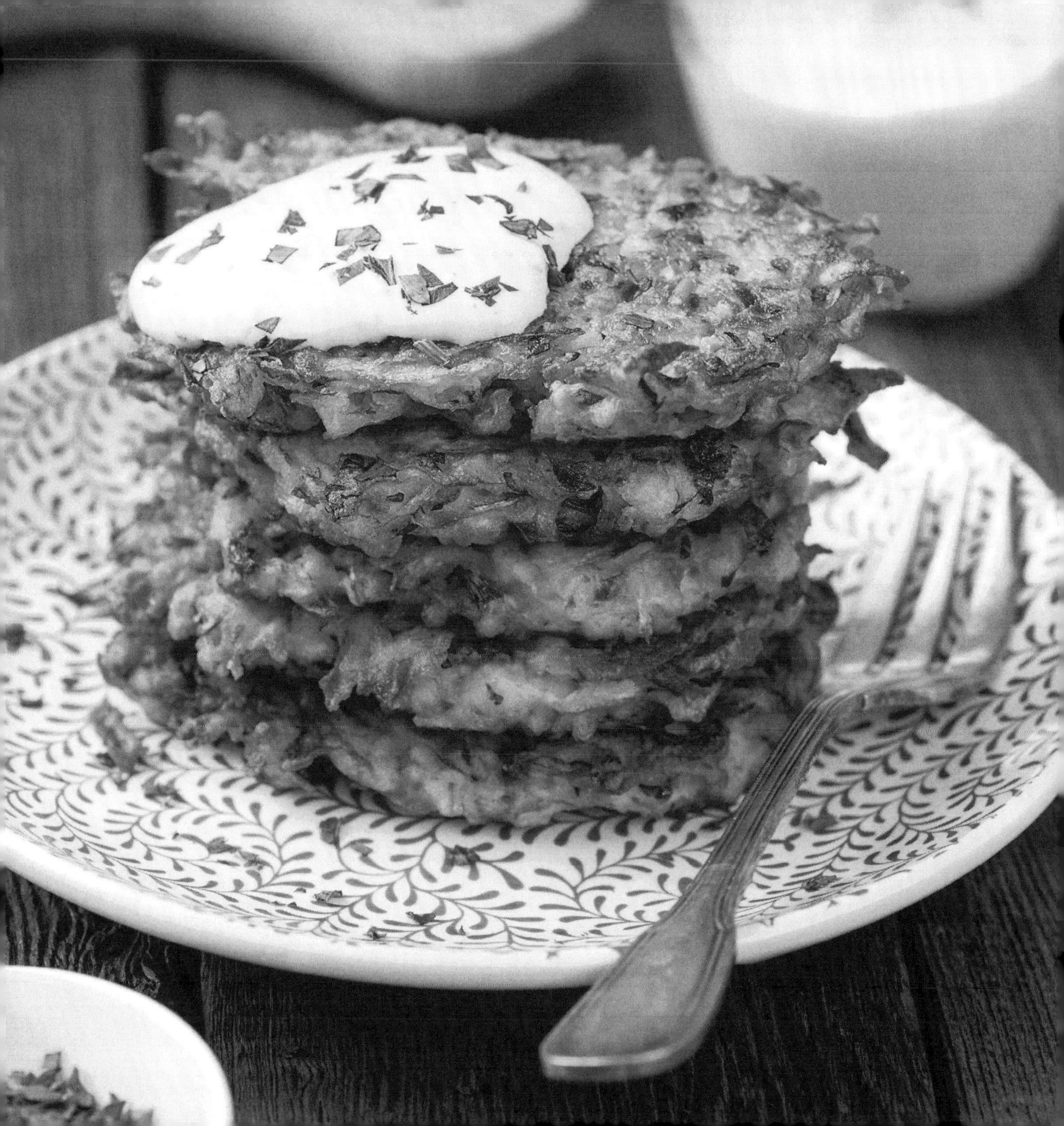

Breakfast Sausage Patties

A tasty way to start the day, these sausage patties are perfect for breakfast or brunch. Double the recipe and freeze half patties so you have them already prepared for next time!

Servings: 12 Patties   Prep Time: 20 Minutes   Cook Time: 20 Minutes

Ingredients

- 2.2 lbs. ground pork
- 2 tablespoons maple syrup
- 1 1/2 teaspoons salt
- 1 teaspoon ground black pepper
- 1 teaspoon garlic powder
- 3/4 teaspoons dried thyme
- 1/2 teaspoon dried sage

Directions

1. To make the sausage meat, place all the ingredients in a large bowl. Then use your hands to mix and combine well.
2. Divide the meat into 12 pieces. Shape each into a ball then gently press into a patty shape between your palms. (If you do not wish to use all the meat, then you can freeze them at this stage)
3. Heat a little oil in a non-stick skillet over medium-high heat. Add the patties (you might need to do it in batches) and cook on each side for about 3 - 4 minutes, or until browned. (To check if the patty is cooked use a thermometer to check that the internal temperature of each patty is 160°F / 71°C).
4. If you are cooking from frozen, follow the instructions above and increase the cooking time by a couple of minutes and ensure the patties are properly cooked through.
5. Serve with bread and some fresh veggies.

NUTRITIONAL INFO: CALORIES: 254 | SODIUM: 339MG | DIETARY FIBER: 0.1G
TOTAL FAT: 2.9G | TOTAL CARBS: 2.6G | PROTEIN: 21.8G.

Crispy Ham and Cheese Waffles

These savory waffles are such a treat that you'll have the whole family asking for more!

Servings: 12 Waffles   **Prep Time: 20 Minutes**   **Cook Time: 35 Minutes**

Ingredients

1 3/4 cups flour
1 tablespoon sugar
2 teaspoons baking powder
1 teaspoon baking soda
1 teaspoon salt
3 large eggs (separated)
1 cup (2 sticks) butter, melted
1 cup buttermilk
3/4 cups soda water
Non-stick vegetable oil spray
1 cup strips of ham, thinly sliced
3/4 cups cheddar cheese, grated
Maple syrup

Directions

1. Preheat the oven to 300°F. Turn on the waffle iron to heat up.
2. In a large bowl, mix the flour, sugar, baking powder, baking soda, and salt.
3. Beat egg whites in a bowl until medium-soft peaks form - if you have an electric whisk it will make this task easier!
4. In a separate bowl, whisk egg yolks, melted butter, buttermilk, and soda water. Gradually whisk in the dry ingredients then fold in the egg whites.
5. Coat the waffle iron with a little non-stick vegetable oil spray to prevent the batter sticking.
6. Pour a little batter onto the waffle iron, making sure it spreads all the way into corners.
7. Scatter a tablespoon each of ham and cheese over the batter. Cook until golden brown and cooked all the way through.
8. Place cooked waffles on a baking sheet and keep them warm in the oven until they are all ready.
9. Serve the waffles with butter and maple syrup.

NUTRITIONAL INFO: CALORIES: 284 | SODIUM: 532MG | DIETARY FIBER: 0.7G
TOTAL FAT: 20.3G | TOTAL CARBS: 18.2G | PROTEIN: 7.9G.

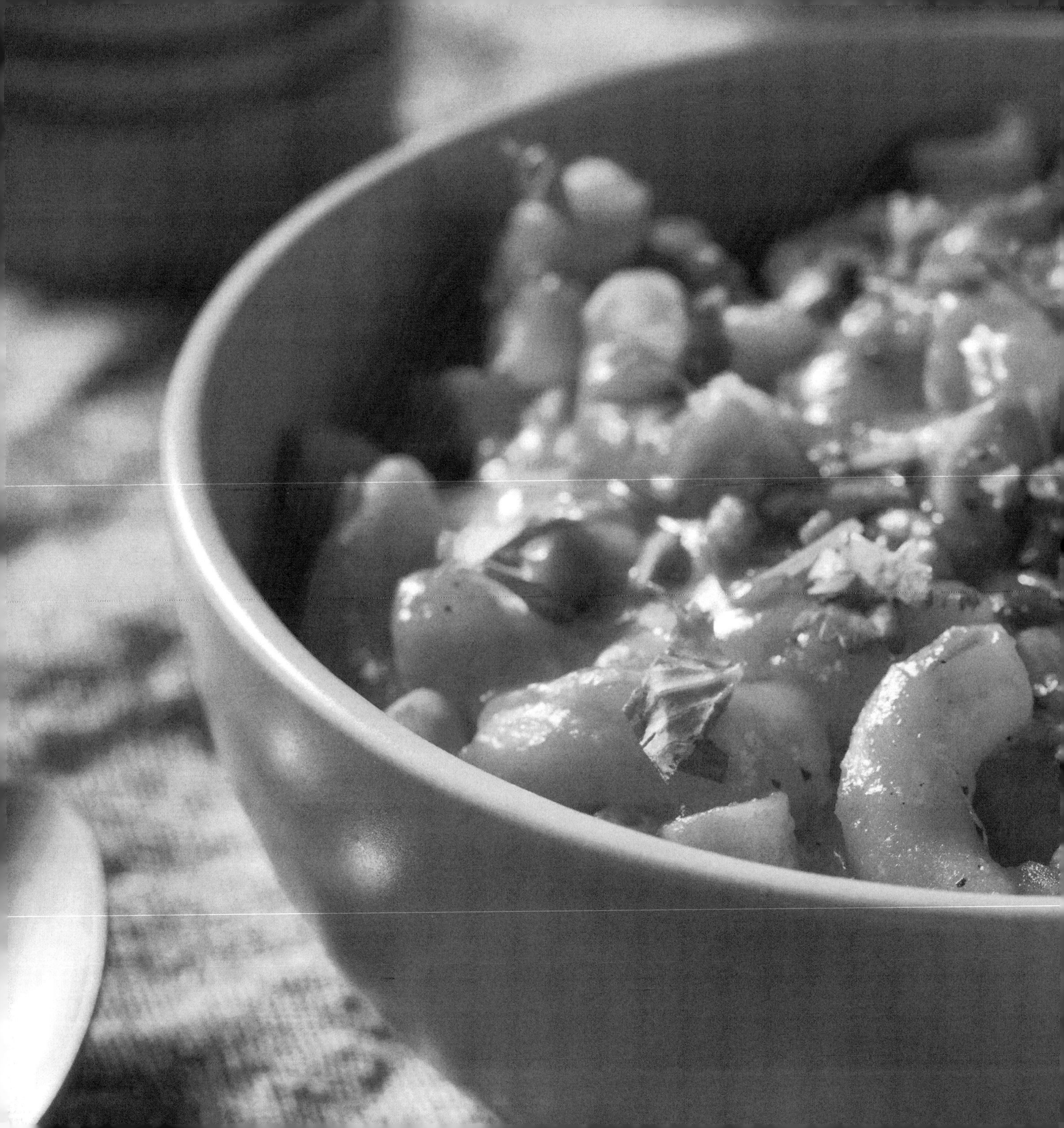

CHAPTER 7
Lunchtime and Snacks

Chili Mac and Cheese

This combo of flavors is bound to be a big hit. Healthy, hearty and quick to make - ticks all the boxes!

Servings: 10   Prep Time: 20 Minutes   Cook Time: 20 Minutes

Ingredients

8 ounces whole-wheat elbow pasta or lentil/chickpea pasta

1/2 tablespoon extra-virgin olive oil

1 red onion, diced

5 cloves garlic, minced

2 - 3 tablespoons chili powder

2 teaspoon ground cumin

1 teaspoon ancho chili powder

3 yellow bell peppers, diced

6-oz baby spinach, shredded

1 cup frozen corn

1 1/2 teaspoons salt or to taste

1 (15-oz) can fire roasted diced tomatoes

1 (15-oz) can black beans, drained and rinsed

1 (15-oz) can kidney beans, drained and rinsed

1 (15 oz) can tomato sauce

2 cups Mexican shredded cheese blend

2 cups vegetable broth

Directions

1. Bring a large pot of water to a boil, add a splash of olive oil and a little salt. Cook the pasta according to the directions on the package and set to one side.

2. In a separate large pot, add olive oil, onion, garlic and spices. Sauté until the onions have slightly caramelized, approximately 5 to 10 minutes on a medium heat.

3. Then add the peppers, spinach, corn, salt, diced tomatoes, black beans, kidney beans and sauté for another 5 to 10 minutes on a medium heat.

4. Add half of the can of tomato sauce and stir to combine. Then add in the pasta and cheese, give it a good stir to combine.

5. If the mixture is a little dry, then add in the rest of the tomato sauce. Add 1/2 cup vegetable broth at a time until the sauce is a good consistency. Serve and enjoy!

NUTRITIONAL INFO: CALORIES: 288 | SODIUM: 553MG | DIETARY FIBER: 13.4G
TOTAL FAT: 5.5G | TOTAL CARBS: 46.3G | PROTEIN: 18G.

Easy Spinach Pesto and Pasta

Spinach Pesto is one of the best ways to serve greens to kids. Easy to make, this quick family dinner hits the spot every time!

Servings: 8   **Prep Time: 10 Minutes**   **Cook Time: 10 Minutes**

Ingredients

1 lb. or 4 cups dry pasta

2 cups peas, frozen

4 cups lightly packed baby spinach

1/3 cup olive oil

Juice of 1 lemon

1/2 cup parmesan, grated

1/2 cup roasted sunflower seeds

Directions

1. Read the package instructions and cook the pasta accordingly.
2. Meanwhile, thaw the frozen peas.
3. For the pesto sauce, place the remaining ingredients from spinach to sunflower seeds in a food processor. Blend until desired consistency is achieved. If desired, season with salt.
4. Stir in the pasta and pesto sauce and add the peas.

NUTRITIONAL INFO: CALORIES: 333 | SODIUM: 112MG | DIETARY FIBER: 4.2G
TOTAL FAT: 13.3G | TOTAL CARBS: 44.1G | PROTEIN: 12.5G.

Cheesy Bean Quesadillas

A classic mix of beans, corn and cheese make these a favorite with kids. A great option for an easy lunch that will never fail to make little tummies happy!

Servings: 8   Prep Time: 10 Minutes   Cook Time: 35 Minutes

Ingredients

4 tablespoons olive oil

10 (8 inches) flour tortillas

16 ounces shredded Mexican cheese blend

1 (15 ounce) can black beans, drained and rinsed

1 (12 ounce) can sweetcorn, drained

1 (7 ounce) can salsa verde

Directions

1. Preheat the oven to 425°F. Grease a baking sheet with 2 tablespoons of the olive oil, use a pastry brush to spread it evenly over the sheet.

2. Place 6 tortillas on the sheet. Make sure there are no gaps on the sheet, there should be 2 tortillas in the middle of the tray and the rest round the sides with half of each hanging over the edge (Note: the overhanging side will be folded over later).

3. Sprinkle half of the cheese over the tortillas (don't put cheese on the part that is hanging over the edge).

4. Next, sprinkle the black beans and corn over the cheese, then put dollops of salsa verde evenly spread across the tortillas. Finally, cover with the rest of the cheese.

5. Fold over the overhanging edges of the tortillas then put the remaining 2 tortillas over the middle tortillas. Drizzle the last of the olive oil over the top.

6. Take a second baking sheet and place on top of the tortillas and press a little to flatten.

7. Place the quesadillas with both baking sheets in the oven and bake for 20 minutes then remove the top baking sheet and continue to bake for a further 10 to 15 minutes until golden-brown.

8. Cut the quesadillas into 8 equal squares, serve and enjoy.

NUTRITIONAL INFO: CALORIES: 484 | SODIUM: 1208MG | DIETARY FIBER: 6.3G
TOTAL FAT: 21.1G | TOTAL CARBS: 46.3G | PROTEIN: 24.6G.

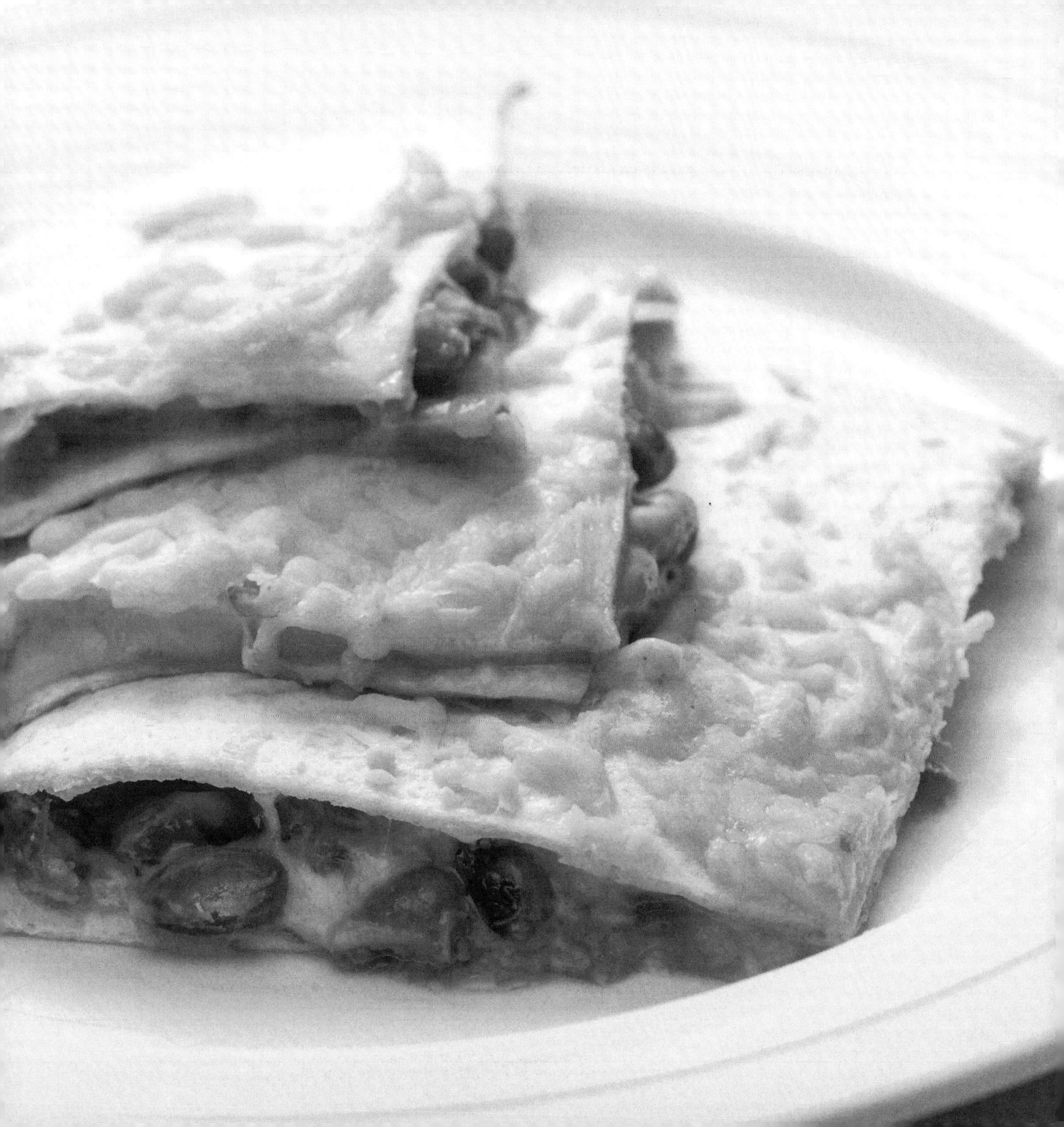

Quinoa Chicken Strips

Kids beware, eat these tasty little chicken strips quick before mom and dad pinch take them all!

Servings: 6   Prep Time: 15 Minutes   Cook Time: 12 - 15 Minutes

Ingredients

3/4 cups all-purpose flour

1 teaspoon garlic powder

1 1/4 teaspoons salt

3/4 teaspoons freshly ground black pepper

2 eggs

2 cups quinoa, cooked

2 lbs. chicken breast, cut into bite-size strips

Cooking spray or a little olive oil

TO SERVE:

Honey mustard

Barbecue sauce

Directions

1. Preheat the oven to 400°F. Grease and line a baking sheet.
2. Prepare three shallow sided medium sized bowls, in the first mix the flour, garlic powder, salt and black pepper. Crack the eggs into the second bowl and whisk slightly. Put the cooked quinoa into the third bowl.
3. Take one strip of chicken at a time and dip in the flour mixture until fully coated. Then put the floured strip into the egg, lift out and let the excess drip off. Finally roll in the quinoa ensuring it's fully coated.
4. Place the strip on the prepared baking sheet and repeat stage 3 with the remaining chicken strips.
5. Drizzle the chicken strips with a little olive oil or spray with cooking spray.
6. Bake in the oven for 6 to 8 minutes, then flip the strips and cook for a further 6 to 8 minutes until fully cooked through and golden brown.
7. Before serving, season with a little salt and pepper. Then serve with your choice of dipping sauces.

NUTRITIONAL INFO: CALORIES: 461 | SODIUM: 586MG | DIETARY FIBER: 4.5G
TOTAL FAT: 8.8G | TOTAL CARBS: 48.9G | PROTEIN: 43.6G.

Crispy Bacon Pasta Salad

Make ahead and store in the fridge for when you need it. These fresh veggies, pasta and bacon make for a really yummy lunch!

Servings: 8   Prep Time: 10 Minutes   Cook Time: 10 Minutes

Ingredients

1 lb. bacon
1 lb. dry pasta
1 1/2 cups ranch dressing
2 cups cherry tomatoes, halved
3 cups shredded romaine lettuce
2 avocados peeled, pitted and diced
2 tablespoons parsley chopped

Directions

1. Fry the bacon until crisp then crumble and set aside.
2. Prepare a pan of boiling, salted water and cook pasta according to package directions.
3. Drain the pasta in a colander then run under cold water until cool.
4. Transfer the pasta to a large bowl and toss with the ranch dressing. Add the crumbled bacon, cherry tomatoes, lettuce and avocado. Mix gently and make sure everything is evenly coated with the dressing.
5. Top with a sprinkle of parsley and serve immediately.

NUTRITIONAL INFO: CALORIES: 364 | SODIUM: 611MG | DIETARY FIBER: 3.7G
TOTAL FAT: 13G | TOTAL CARBS: 40.0G | PROTEIN: 22G.

Turkey Roll-ups

These tasty roll-ups are full of flavor and are a great way to get little ones to eat salad! They make the perfect lunch box fillers or are great for sharing at a picnic.

Servings: 1   Prep Time: 10 Minutes   Cook Time: No Cooking

Ingredients

1 tortilla, or more if making for more

1 teaspoon spreadable cream cheese

1 teaspoon pesto

3 – 4 thin slices turkey

1 slice of cheese

1 handful romaine salad

Directions

1. Lay the tortilla flat on a cutting board. Evenly spread the cream cheese, then spread over the pesto.
2. Next, place the turkey slices over 2/3 of the tortilla. Then add on the slice of cheese.
3. Place the salad leaves in a line down the middle.
4. Then roll up the tortilla tightly, being careful to make sure none of the fillings escape.
5. Cut the roll into 5 pieces and serve or store in an airtight container for later.

NUTRITIONAL INFO: CALORIES: 288 | SODIUM: 350MG | DIETARY FIBER: 2.1G
TOTAL FAT: 13.9G | TOTAL CARBS: 14.2G | PROTEIN: 25.7G.

Homemade Fish Fingers

Fish is a great source of protein and making your own fish fingers ensures only the best of ingredients are used. Get little ones to help with the dipping - it's sure to be messy but lots of fun!

Servings: 4   Prep Time: 10 Minutes   Cook Time: 15 Minutes

Ingredients

1 egg

1/4 cup milk

400 g white fish cut into finger-sized strips

1/2 cup plain flour

Salt and pepper

2 cups breadcrumbs

Olive oil spray

Directions

1. Preheat the oven to 400°F.
2. Prepare 3 medium sized, shallow sided bowls. In the first whisk together the egg and milk. Put the flour in the second bowl, season with a little salt and pepper and stir to combine. Put the breadcrumbs in the third bowl.
3. Start by dipping the fish in flour, then dip in egg mixture, and finally roll in the breadcrumbs.
4. Place the breaded fish slices on a baking tray and spray with a little oil.
5. Bake in the oven for 15 minutes until golden brown and fully cooked through.

NUTRITIONAL INFO: CALORIES: 417 | SODIUM: 400MG | DIETARY FIBER: 1.6G
TOTAL FAT: 5.1G | TOTAL CARBS: 56.8G | PROTEIN: 33.1G.

Make-it-Yourself Sushi

Make mealtime a cooking class with this delicious vegetarian sushi. Make sure to keep the pieces of bamboo in the rolling mat horizontal as rolling is done easiest from bottom to top.

Servings: 6   Prep Time: 10 Minutes   Cook Time: 20 Minutes

Ingredients

2 cups sushi rice

1/2 cup rice vinegar

3 bell peppers, 1 red, 1 orange, and 1 yellow, all sliced thinly

1 carrot, peeled and julienned

1 mango, thinly sliced

1 avocado, thinly sliced

1 cucumber, sliced into thin strips

1/2 cup shredded purple cabbage

1/2 cup beets, cooked and sliced into thin strips

1/2 cup rice vinegar

6 nori seaweed wraps

TO SERVE:

Soy sauce

Pickled ginger

Wasabi

Directions

1. In a large pan put the sushi rice with 4 cups of water. Stir well then cover with a tightly fitting lid and bring to a boil. Once it is boiling then reduce the temperature and allow to simmer for 10 minutes. Then remove from the heat, let sit for a further 10 minutes, making sure not to remove the lid.
2. While the rice is cooking, prepare the vegetables by slicing them as finely as possible.
3. Once the rice is ready, stir in the rice vinegar, then put into a bowl to cool down slightly.
4. Let the rolling commence: Start by placing a seaweed sheet onto a bamboo rolling mat.
5. Have a bowl of warm water nearby so you can wet your hands a little, then place a little rice on the seaweed sheet. Carefully pat it into a thin even layer to cover the whole sheet.
6. Add some of the vegetables to make the filling. Be sure to place the vegetables in a line about 1/3 of the way in from the bottom of the sheet.
7. Then start to roll the bamboo mat up, starting with the bottom edge. As you roll, squeeze the bamboo mat tightly to make a well rolled sushi roll.
8. Slice the roll into pieces using a sharp knife.
9. Serve with the soy sauce, ginger and wasabi.

NUTRITIONAL INFO: CALORIES: 502 | SODIUM: 247MG | DIETARY FIBER: 6.7G
TOTAL FAT: 7.4G | TOTAL CARBS: 94.6G | PROTEIN: 9.8G.

Mini Muffins with a Difference

Every kid loves muffins and hot dogs - so here's a sure-fire way to impress little ones by combining two of their favorite things and making them a kiddie friendly size too!

Servings: 48 Mini Muffins   Prep Time: 15 Minutes   Cook Time: 8 - 12 Minutes

Ingredients

1/2 cup butter, melted

1/2 cup sugar

2 eggs

1 cup buttermilk

1/2 teaspoon baking soda

1 cup cornmeal

1 cup all-purpose flour

1/2 teaspoon salt

8 - 10 beef hot dogs, cut into 1" pieces

Directions

1. Preheat the oven to 375°F.
2. In a large bowl, whisk the butter and sugar together.
3. Add one egg at a time, whisking continuously until well combined.
4. Next, add in the buttermilk and whisk again.
5. In a separate bowl, add the baking soda, cornmeal, flour, and salt, give a quick stir, then gradually whisk in a little of the flour mixture at a time to the wet ingredients to make a soft batter.
6. Prepare a mini muffin tin by spraying a little non-stick spray into each cup. Then put 1 tablespoon of the batter into each cup.
7. In each cup, put a piece of hot dog into the middle of the batter.
8. Bake in the oven for 8 - 12 minutes or until the top is golden brown.
9. Allow to cool in the tin for 5 minutes transferring to a wire rack.
10. Serve warm or cool. Keep any leftovers in the refrigerator. The mini muffins can be reheated in the microwave for 20 seconds before serving.

NUTRITIONAL INFO: CALORIES: 70 | SODIUM: 144MG | DIETARY FIBER: 0.3G
TOTAL FAT: 3.8G | TOTAL CARBS: 6.5G | PROTEIN: 2.6G.

Roasted Broccoli and Cheese Toastie

This combo works surprisingly well in a grilled sandwich. A perfect way to get little ones to enjoy their broccoli!

Servings: 4 Sandwiches   **Prep Time: 5 Minutes**   **Cook Time: 15 Minutes**

Ingredients

- 1 medium (1/2 lb.) head broccoli, chopped into small florets
- 2 tablespoons olive oil
- 1/2 teaspoon salt
- 1/4 teaspoon black pepper
- 8 slices bread
- 2 tablespoons unsalted butter, softened
- 1 cup cheddar cheese, grated

Directions

1. Preheat the oven to 400°F.
2. Put the broccoli florets on to a baking tray, trickle over the oil, salt, and pepper, then toss to combine. Roast in the oven for 8 to 10 minutes, then put to one side to cool.
3. Put 4 slices of bread on a board. Butter one side of the bread then turn over and put the buttered side down on the board.
4. Add a layer of grated cheese then add the roasted broccoli and top with another layer of cheese.
5. Place a slice of bread on top then butter the outside.
6. Heat a frying pan or skillet. Place the sandwich in the pan, cook each side for 3 to 4 minutes until the cheese has melted and the bread is nicely browned.
7. Serve immediately.

NUTRITIONAL INFO: CALORIES: 287 | SODIUM: 675MG | DIETARY FIBER: 1.9G
TOTAL FAT: 22.7G | TOTAL CARBS: 11.7G | PROTEIN: 9.2G.

Chicken and Quinoa Meaty Muffins

A delicious and healthy lunch option bursting with flavor. Serve with a fresh green salad and enjoy!

Servings: 12 Muffins or 6 Servings **Prep Time: 25 Minutes** **Cook Time: 25 Minutes**

Ingredients

FOR THE QUINOA:

2/3 cups water

1/3 cup uncooked quinoa

FOR THE MUFFINS:

1 teaspoon olive oil

4 cloves of garlic, crushed

1/2 cup yellow onion, finely chopped

1 red or orange pepper, finely diced

1 teaspoon cumin

1 teaspoon dried oregano

1 teaspoon chili powder, optional

Few dashes hot sauce, optional

Few dashes red pepper flakes, optional

1/2 cup chopped cilantro

Salt and black pepper, to taste

3/4 cups red enchilada sauce

1 lb. ground chicken or lean ground turkey breast

1 egg

2/3 cups Colby jack or Mexican cheese, grated

Directions

1. Start by preparing the quinoa: Put the water in a small saucepan, add the quinoa and bring to a boil. Once the water is boiling put a lid on the pan to cover, turn down the heat and allow to simmer for approximately 15 minutes or until all of the water has been absorbed. Then remove from the heat, and use a fork fluff up the quinoa.

2. Preheat the oven to 350°F. Use cooking spray to prepare a 12-cup muffin tin.

3. In a medium sized frying pan, heat the olive oil then add the garlic, onion, and pepper. Cook for a couple of minutes until the onions have softened. Then transfer to a large bowl and allow to cool for a few minutes.

4. Once the onion and peppers have cooled, add the cooked quinoa, cumin, and oregano. If using chili powder, hot sauce, and red pepper flakes, add these in now. Finally add in the cilantro, salt and pepper and half of the enchilada sauce.

5. Next add in the ground chicken (or turkey), egg and half of the cheese. Use your hands to mix, making sure that all ingredients are well combined.

6. Use an ice cream scoop to scoop out even sized amounts of the mixture and place the scoops into the prepared muffin cups.

7. Bake in the oven for 25 - 30 minutes, then remove and spoon the remaining enchilada sauce and cheese over the top of each muffin.

8. Put back in the oven and bake for another 5 minutes until the cheese is melted and muffins are cooked through.

9. Allow to cool for a few minutes then serve with a green salad.

NUTRITIONAL INFO: CALORIES: 161 | SODIUM: 228MG | DIETARY FIBER: 0.9G
TOTAL FAT: 8.2G | TOTAL CARBS: 6.1G | PROTEIN: 15.1G.

Cheesy Meatball Frittata

Delicious, heartwarming and nutritious, this dish is best served with a green salad.

Servings: 4   Prep Time: 15 Minutes   Cook Time: 25 Minutes

Ingredients

1 tablespoon olive oil
2 garlic cloves, crushed
1 cup cherry tomatoes, halved
Salt and pepper
8 eggs
2 tablespoons Parmigiano- Reggiano, grated
2 tablespoons fresh basil, chopped
1/2 lb. cooked meatballs, halved
4 ounces mozzarella, cut into 1/2-inch pieces

Directions

1. Preheat the oven to 425°F.
2. Put a large ovenproof frying pan or skillet on a medium-high heat, add 1/2 tablespoon olive oil.
3. Add in the crushed garlic and cook for one minute. Add the cherry tomatoes and a pinch of salt. Cook for 3 to 4 minutes, then pour the tomatoes on to a plate making sure to scrape all of the juices onto the plate too.
4. In a bowl, whisk the eggs then stir in the Parmigiano and basil. Season with salt and pepper.
5. Put the pan back on the heat with 1/2 tablespoon of olive oil. Place the meatballs and tomatoes in the base of the pan.
6. Pour the egg mixture over the meatballs and sprinkle the mozzarella across the pan as evenly as possible.
7. Cook until the edges of the frittata are starting to set. Then use a spatula to pull the edges away from the sides of the pan a little in order to let the raw egg flow behind. Go round the pan and do this on all sides. Continue to cook for 5 minutes until the eggs are set around the edge of the pan.
8. Place the pan in the oven and bake for 5 to 10 minutes until the eggs are nicely set in the center and the top is browned.
9. Remove the pan from the oven and rest for 5 more minutes, then use a spatula to loosen the sides then slide the frittata onto a board.
10. Serve immediately and enjoy!

NUTRITIONAL INFO: CALORIES: 371 | SODIUM: 582MG | DIETARY FIBER: 1.3G
TOTAL FAT: 26.2G | TOTAL CARBS: 8G | PROTEIN: 30.5G.

Tuna Bean Jacket Potatoes

Jacket potatoes are always a winner and with this colorful and super tasty filling, they'll definitely be number 1!

Servings: 4   Prep Time: 10 Minutes   Cook Time: 1 Hour

Ingredients

4 baking potatoes
1 can cannellini beans
200g tin tuna in water, drained and flaked
1 pepper, any color, deseeded and chopped
2 tomatoes, chopped
4 spring onions, finely chopped
2 teaspoons red or white wine vinegar
2 teaspoons tomato purée
1 pinch ground black pepper

Directions

1. Preheat the oven 400°F.
2. Put the potatoes in an ovenproof baking tray, prick all over with a fork then bake for 1 hour until fully cooked and soft in the center.
3. While the potatoes bake, in a bowl, mix the cannellini beans with the tuna, pepper, tomatoes, spring onions, vinegar and tomato purée. Season with the ground black pepper.
4. Once the potatoes are cooked, place each one on a plate, then split down the middle and squeeze the sides slightly to push up the soft potato. Spoon over the bean and tuna mixture and serve immediately.

NUTRITIONAL INFO: CALORIES: 257 | SODIUM: 79MG | DIETARY FIBER: 6.4G
TOTAL FAT: 2G | TOTAL CARBS: 43.7G | PROTEIN: 30.4G.

Creamy Chickpea Curry

To save time use frozen onions, garlic and ginger. Serve with microwave rice if in a rush.

Servings: 4   Prep Time: 5 Minutes   Cook Time: 20 Minutes

Ingredients

1/2 tablespoon oil
1 medium onion, finely chopped
1 clove garlic, crushed
1 teaspoon ginger, finely chopped
3 teaspoons curry paste
2 cans chickpeas, drained
1 can chopped tomatoes
1 can coconut milk
Rice and chopped fresh coriander to serve

Directions

1. In a large frying pan, heat the oil, then add the onions, garlic and ginger and fry for 4 to 5 minutes on a medium high heat.
2. Stir in the curry paste and cook for a further minute.
3. Then add the chickpeas, chopped tomatoes and coconut milk. Stir well and bring to a boil, then reduce the heat and simmer for 15 minutes.
4. Serve with rice and chopped coriander.

NUTRITIONAL INFO: CALORIES: 385 | SODIUM: 18MG | DIETARY FIBER: 8.8G
TOTAL FAT: 24.8G | TOTAL CARBS: 33.9G | PROTEIN: 10G.

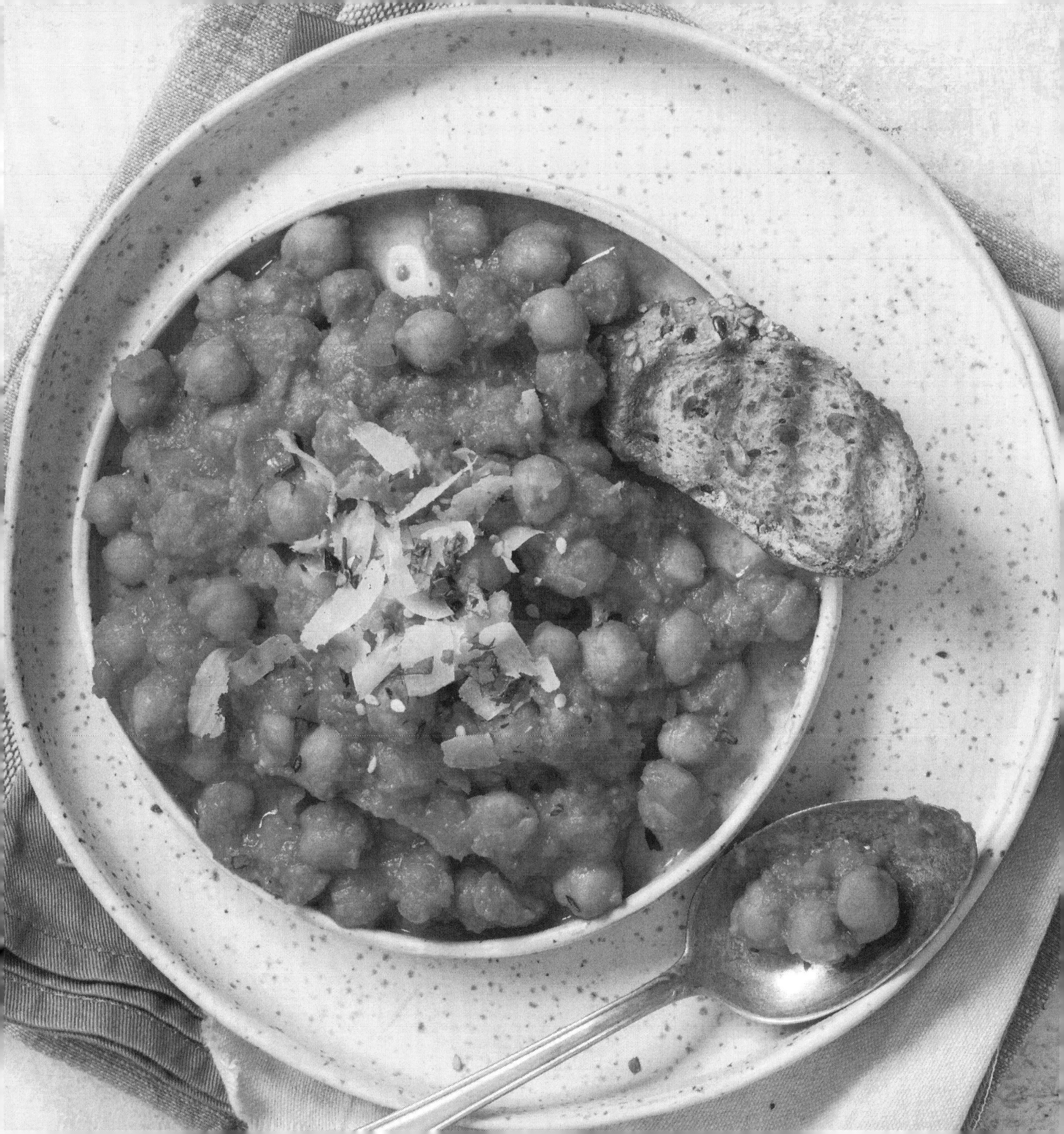

Gluten Free Granola Bars

These granola bars are the perfect healthy snack. Sweet and chewy, don't expect these to last for long!

Servings: 12 Bars   Prep Time: 10 Minutes   Cook Time: None

Ingredients

2 cups gluten free rolled oats
1/2 cup gluten free oat flour
2 cups gluten free crisp rice cereal
1/2 cup unsweetened coconut chips
4 tablespoons virgin coconut oil
1 cup light brown sugar
1/2 teaspoon salt
1/2 cup honey
1 teaspoon vanilla extract

Directions

1. Line an 8-inch square baking tray with parchment paper.
2. Put the rolled oats, oat flour, rice cereal and coconut chips in a large bowl and stir well to combine.
3. Place the coconut oil and brown sugar in a saucepan on a medium heat, sprinkle in the salt. Stir from time to time and cook until the mixture becomes a liquid and the sugar is melted and combined. Bring to a simmer then allow to cook for another 45 seconds without stirring it.
4. Remove from the heat and then stir in the honey and vanilla. Keep stirring until the mixture comes off the boil. Leave to cool for a few minutes.
5. Next, pour the warm mixture into the dry ingredients and mix really well until thoroughly combined.
6. Tip into the prepared baking tray, spread out the mixture over the whole tray and press down firmly.
7. Place in the refrigerator to cool and set.
8. Once set, tip onto a chopping board and use a sharp knife to cut into 12 slim rectangles.
9. Serve and enjoy. Any leftovers can be stored in an airtight container.

NUTRITIONAL INFO: CALORIES: 285 | SODIUM: 148MG | DIETARY FIBER: 3.5G
TOTAL FAT: 12.2G | TOTAL CARBS: 41.5G | PROTEIN: 3.9G.

Veggie Stacks

Fresh, tasty and gluten free, this lovely little combo is perfect as a healthy snack and takes almost no time at all to prepare.

Servings: 4   Prep Time: 5 Minutes   Cook Time: None

Ingredients

1 cucumber
1 tomato
1 avocado
1/4 lb. sliced chicken or turkey
1/4 lb. sliced cheese
1/4 teaspoon sea salt

Directions

1. Prepare the vegetable by slicing the cucumber, tomato, and avocado into 1/4-inch-thick slices.

2. Use a toothpick to build your stacks: start and finish with a slice of cucumber and layer up the rest of the ingredients in between in any order. Folding up the sliced meat and cheese into 1-inch sized squares will help them to stay on the toothpick better.

3. Sprinkle with a little sea salt and enjoy!

NUTRITIONAL INFO: CALORIES: 279 | SODIUM: 318MG | DIETARY FIBER: 3.9G
TOTAL FAT: 20.7G | TOTAL CARBS: 8G | PROTEIN: 16.9G.

Strawberry Rolls

This recipe is best made just before you go to bed so that it can sit in the oven overnight.

Servings: 8   Prep Time: 20 Minutes   Cook Time: 8 Hours

Ingredients

4 cups strawberries, washed and husks removed

1 tablespoon sugar

1/2 cup water

Coconut oil spray

Directions

1. Put the strawberries, sugar and water in a food processor and blend until smooth.
2. Pour the mixture into a saucepan, bring to a simmer and allow to cook for 10 - 15 minutes.
3. Prepare a large baking sheet by spraying with a little coconut oil spray, then pour in the strawberry mixture, tilt the tray to ensure the mixture is evenly spread across the whole tray.
4. Set the oven to 140°F and place the tray in the oven for 8 hours, during this time the mixture will dehydrate and become solid.
5. Remove from the oven, allow to cool and slice into 8 squares, roll up and enjoy!

NUTRITIONAL INFO: CALORIES: 29 | SODIUM: 1MG | DIETARY FIBER: 1.4G
TOTAL FAT: 0.2G | TOTAL CARBS: 7G | PROTEIN: 0.5G.

Baked Cinnamon and Apple Rings

This is a lovely little homemade snack that little ones will love. You can store the baked apple rings in an airtight container for up to a week.

Servings: 3 - 4   Prep Time: 5 Minutes   Cook Time: 3 Hours

Ingredients

3 apples, any variety will do
1 tablespoon ground cinnamon
2 tablespoons granulated sugar

Directions

1. Preheat the oven to 200°F and line two large baking sheets with parchment paper.
2. Core the apples using an apple corer. Then thinly slice the apples into 3mm thick rings.
3. Spread the apple rings out across the baking sheets in a single layer.
4. Mix the cinnamon and sugar together in a small bowl, then evenly sprinkle over the apple rings.
5. Bake in the oven for 1 hour, then turn the apple rings over and bake for a further 1 to 1 1/2 hours.
6. Turn the oven off but leave the apples inside for another hour. This will make them crunchy!
7. Allow to cool a little more before serving.

NUTRITIONAL INFO: CALORIES: 114 | SODIUM: 2MG | DIETARY FIBER: 5G
TOTAL FAT: 0.3G | TOTAL CARBS: 30.5G | PROTEIN: 0.5G.

Shaped Crackers

These crackers are gluten free and suitable for vegans. Get little ones involved in rolling out the dough and cutting the dough into different shapes.

Servings: 12 Crackers   **Prep Time: 15 Minutes**   **Cook Time: 10 Minutes**

Ingredients

- 1 cup gluten free all-purpose white flour
- 1/2 teaspoon baking soda
- 1/2 teaspoon cinnamon
- 2 teaspoons egg replacer
- 2 tablespoons coconut oil, melted
- 1 tablespoon molasses
- 1/2 teaspoon vanilla extract
- 2 - 3 tablespoons iced water
- 1 teaspoon icing sugar for dusting

Directions

1. Preheat the oven to 350°F and line a baking sheet with parchment paper.
2. In a large bowl, sieve in the flour, baking soda and cinnamon. Add in the egg replacer then mix well.
3. Melt the shortening in the microwave then add along with the molasses and vanilla extract to the dry ingredients. Mix all the ingredients together, it will be quite dry and crumbly at this stage.
4. Gradually add in a little of the iced water at a time to bring the mixture together to form a dough.
5. Keep the dough in the bowl and knead by hand for 1 to 2 minutes, the dough should be firm to touch.
6. Place the dough on a piece of parchment paper, press the dough a little to spread it out, then put another piece of parchment paper on top, then roll out to 1/8-inch thickness.
7. Peel the top parchment paper off the dough then using cookie cutters cut the dough into shapes.
8. Place on the prepared baking sheet and bake for 8 - 10 minutes until the edges become golden brown.
9. Place on a wire rack to cool, once they have cooled dust with the icing sugar and serve!

NUTRITIONAL INFO: CALORIES: 39 | SODIUM: 57MG | DIETARY FIBER: 0.2G
TOTAL FAT: 2.4G | TOTAL CARBS: 3.4G | PROTEIN: 0.8G.

Pizza with a Difference

If you love pizza toppings, then this recipe is for you! Gluten free and low carb - the healthy way to eat pizza!

Servings: 12 Pizzas   Prep Time: 10 Minutes   Cook Time: 30 Minutes

Ingredients

36 slices thick-cut Canadian bacon
3/4 cups pizza sauce
1 can pineapple chunks, drained
1 1/2 cups Mozzarella cheese, grated

Directions

1. Preheat the oven to 350°F then lightly grease a regular size 12 cup muffin tin.
2. Arrange 3 pieces of the bacon into each muffin cup so they overlap in the middle, but fully cover the whole cup. Press down slightly.
3. Put 1 tablespoon of pizza sauce on the bacon in each cup.
4. Distribute the pineapple chunks evenly amongst each cup, then top with the cheese.
5. Place in the oven and bake for 25 to 30 minutes until the top is bubbling and golden.
6. Use a fork to remove them from the muffin tin and serve immediately.

NUTRITIONAL INFO: CALORIES: 109 | SODIUM: 804MG | DIETARY FIBER: 0.4G
TOTAL FAT: 3.5G | TOTAL CARBS: 4.7G | PROTEIN: 13.5G.

Mozzarella Sticks

Use gluten free flour and breadcrumbs to make this recipe celiac suitable.

Servings: 12 Sticks   Prep Time: 1 1/2 Hours   Cook Time: 10 Minutes

Ingredients

12 part-skim mozzarella sticks
1 egg, beaten
2 tablespoons all-purpose flour
6 tablespoons breadcrumbs
2 tablespoons grated parmesan cheese

Directions

1. Prepare a baking sheet with parchment paper, cut the mozzarella sticks in half then place on the sheet, pop in the freezer for an hour.
2. Take 3 shallow sided, medium sized bowls. Put the flour in the first, the beaten egg in the second, then mix the breadcrumbs and parmesan cheese together in the third.
3. Take the mozzarella sticks out of the freezer, start by dipping in the flour, then in the egg and then roll in the breadcrumb mix, then place back on the baking sheet.
4. Once all the mozzarella sticks have been dipped and rolled, then place the baking sheet back in the freezer for another 10 minutes.
5. Preheat the oven to 400°F prepare another baking sheet, first line it with foil then spray with non-stick spray.
6. Take the mozzarella sticks out of the freezer, transfer to the foiled tray, then bake in the oven for 3 minutes, flip them over then bake for another 3 minutes.
7. Serve with a dipping sauce of your choice!

NUTRITIONAL INFO: CALORIES: 99 | SODIUM: 217MG | DIETARY FIBER: 0.2G
TOTAL FAT: 5.3G | TOTAL CARBS: 4.2G | PROTEIN: 8.2G.

Sweet Potato Chips

Looking for a tasty yet healthy movie time snack? Then look no further!

Servings: 2   Prep Time: 10 Minutes   Cook Time: 30 Minutes

Ingredients

1 sweet potato
1 tablespoon olive oil or coconut oil
1/2 teaspoon sea salt flakes

Directions

1. Preheat the oven to 375°F
2. Peel the sweet potato and slice into very thin strips.
3. Place the sweet potato strips on a baking sheet, drizzle with olive oil and toss to coat. Then, make sure they are evenly spread across the sheet before putting in the oven.
4. Bake for approximately 30 minutes - turning halfway through, the strips should be crispy but not overcooked.
5. Sprinkle with the sea salt and serve!

NUTRITIONAL INFO: CALORIES: 112 | SODIUM: 115MG | DIETARY FIBER: 1.9G
TOTAL FAT: 7.1G | TOTAL CARBS: 11.8G | PROTEIN: 1.2G.

Carrot and Apple Oatcakes

Healthy and tasty, these oatcakes are a great snack or make the perfect breakfast or brunch item.

Servings: 12   Prep Time: 10 Minutes   Cook Time: 10 Minutes

Ingredients

1 egg
1/2 cup whole wheat flour
1/2 cup rolled oats
1/2 teaspoon baking powder
1/2 teaspoon cinnamon
1/2 - 1 cup milk
1 apple grated
1 carrot grated

Directions

1. In a mixing bowl, whisk the egg.
2. Gradually mix in the flour, oats, baking powder and cinnamon.
3. Keep mixing and add 1/2 cup of milk, grated apple and carrot. If the batter seems a little dry, then add in a little more milk and mix well.
4. Heat a frying pan and put in a small knob of butter, allow to melt and spread over the base of the pan.
5. Drop a tablespoonful of the batter into the pan and cook until small bubbles appear on the surface, flip and then cook on the other side until nicely browned. Repeat until all the batter is cooked.
6. Serve the oatcakes plain or with a little syrup.

NUTRITIONAL INFO: CALORIES: 51 | SODIUM: 19MG | DIETARY FIBER: 1.3G
TOTAL FAT: 1.1G | TOTAL CARBS: 8.9G | PROTEIN: 2.2G.

Sweet Potato & Peanut Butter Muffins

Sweet potato and peanut butter are a great flavor combination, and when baked as mini muffins make for a super healthy, super yummy snack.

Servings: 24 Mini Muffins **Prep Time: 15 Minutes** **Cook Time: 15 Minutes**

Ingredients

1 cup sweet potato, cooked and puréed
1/2 cup peanut butter
1/2 overripe banana mashed
2 eggs
2 tablespoons maple syrup
1 teaspoon vanilla extract
1 1/2 cups almond flour
1 teaspoon baking soda
1/4 teaspoon salt
1 teaspoon cinnamon
1/4 teaspoon nutmeg

Directions

1. Preheat the oven to 350°F. Line a mini muffin tin with mini muffin cases.
2. In a large bowl, add the sweet potato purée, peanut butter, banana, eggs, maple syrup and vanilla extract and beat well.
3. In a small bowl, place the almond flour, baking soda, salt, cinnamon, and nutmeg and stir well.
4. Add a tablespoon full of the dry ingredients at a time to the wet ingredients, mix well until it forms a soft dropping consistency.
5. Put a large teaspoonful of the mixture into the muffin cases.
6. Bake for 13 - 15 minutes or until firm to touch and a toothpick comes out clean when inserted in the middle.
7. Place the muffins on a rack and allow to cool.
8. Serve and enjoy!

NUTRITIONAL INFO: CALORIES: 63 | SODIUM: 109MG | DIETARY FIBER: 0.9G
TOTAL FAT: 3.9G | TOTAL CARBS: 5.1G | PROTEIN: 2.4G.

Tropical Cookies

These cookies are moist, chewy and simply delicious! They are quick to make and store well in an airtight container.

Servings: 16 Cookies   Prep Time: 10 Minutes   Cook Time: 12 - 15 Minutes

Ingredients

- 1 1/2 cups dates, pits removed
- 1/2 cup desiccated coconut
- 1/2 cup rolled oats
- 1/2 cup whole wheat or self-raising flour
- 1 teaspoon baking powder
- 1 teaspoon vanilla essence
- 2 tablespoons coconut oil
- 1 ripe banana
- 1/4 cup milk

Directions

1. Preheat the oven to 350°F and line a large baking sheet with parchment paper.
2. Place all ingredients into a large mixing bowl, mix until well combined and a dough has formed.
3. Use an ice cream scoop to scoop out small balls of the dough, use your hands to roll into rounds, then gently squeeze between your palms to just slightly flatten. Place onto the prepared baking sheet.
4. Put the baking tray into the oven and bake for 12-15 mins, until nicely browned on top.
5. Place on a rack to cool.

NUTRITIONAL INFO: CALORIES: 110 | SODIUM: 4MG | DIETARY FIBER: 2.6G
TOTAL FAT: 4.1G | TOTAL CARBS: 18.6G | PROTEIN: 1.5G.

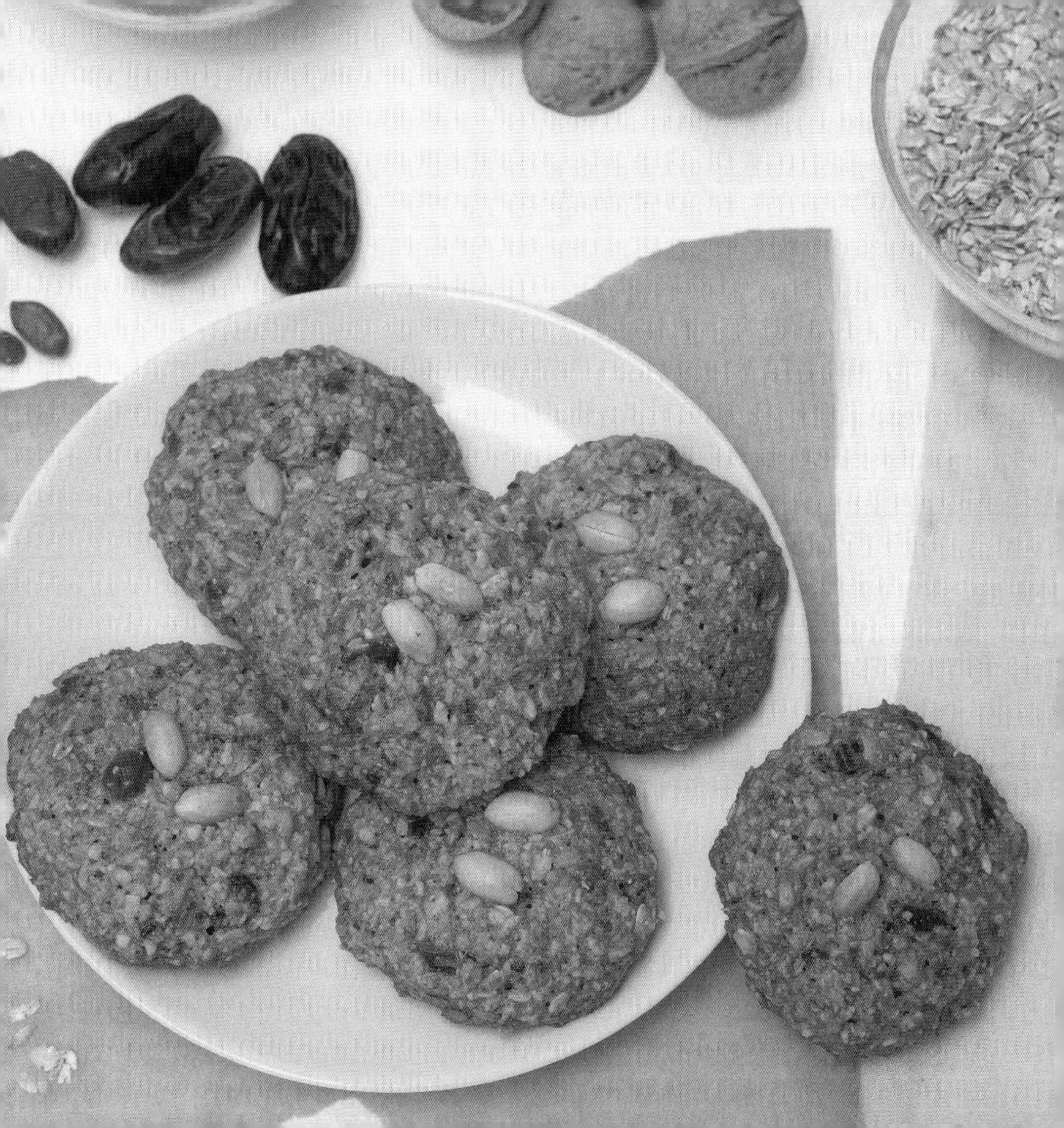

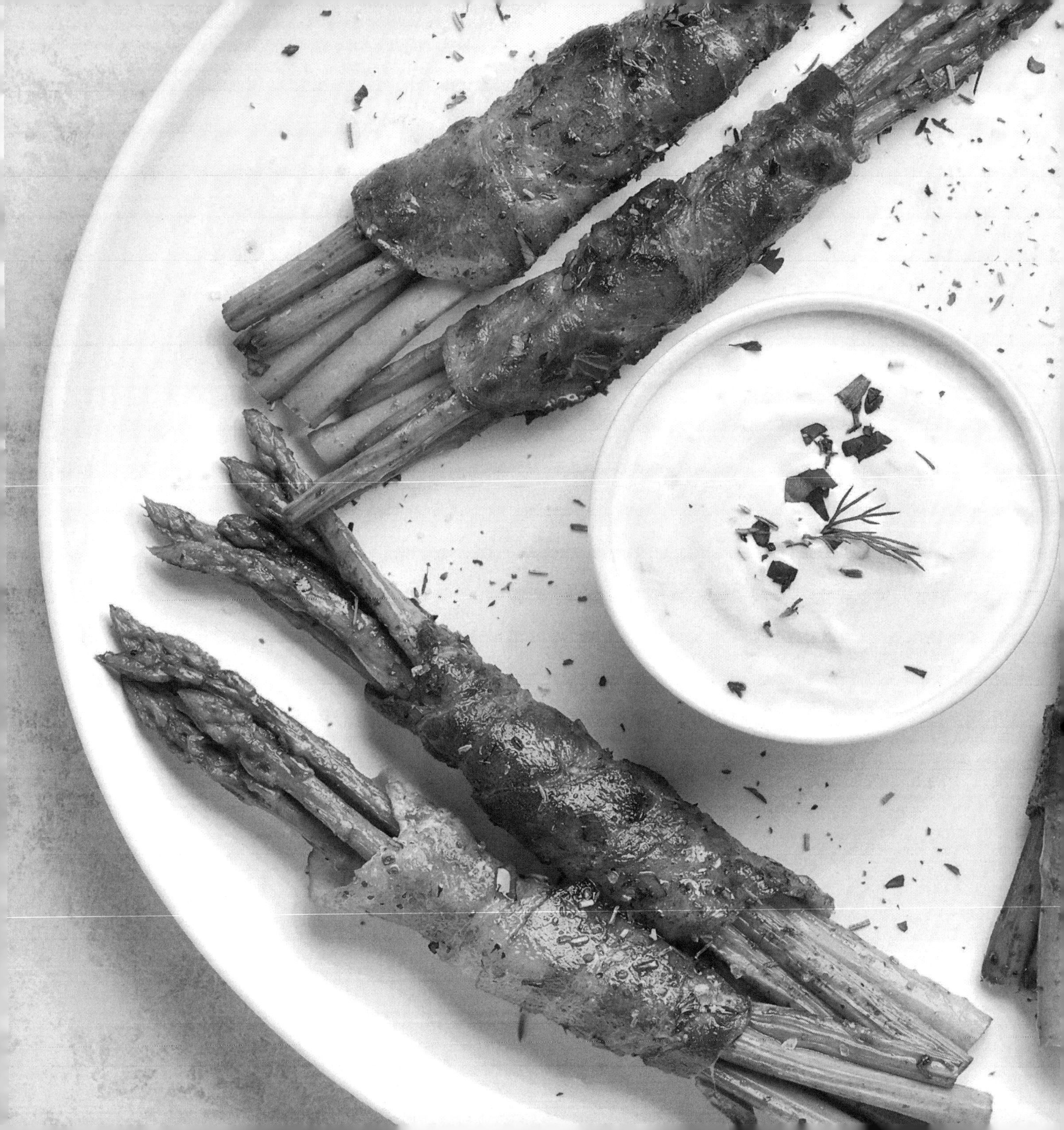

CHAPTER 8
Veggies and Side Dishes

Roasted Broccoli

Adding parmesan cheese and breadcrumbs livens up broccoli and makes this a fantastic side dish to go with any meal.

Servings: 4   Prep Time: 5 Minutes   Cook Time: 25 Minutes

Ingredients

2 medium heads broccoli
4 tablespoons olive oil
3 garlic cloves, minced
1/4 cup parmesan cheese, grated
1/4 cup breadcrumbs
1/2 teaspoon salt
1/4 teaspoon black pepper

Directions

1. Preheat the oven to 400°F and line a large baking sheet with parchment paper.
2. Start by preparing the broccoli heads - wash and cut into small florets then put into a large mixing bowl.
3. Next add the olive oil, garlic, parmesan cheese and breadcrumbs, then mix gently to combine.
4. Season with salt and pepper and finish by giving all the ingredients a good toss to ensure the broccoli is well coated.
5. Transfer the broccoli to the prepared sheet and spread out evenly, if there is any of the breadcrumb mixture left in the bowl, scrape it out and sprinkle over the broccoli.
6. Roast in the oven for 20 to 25 minutes until the broccoli is soft and the top is golden brown.
7. Serve while still hot and enjoy!

NUTRITIONAL INFO: CALORIES: 196 | SODIUM: 546MG | DIETARY FIBER: 1.6G
TOTAL FAT: 16.5G | TOTAL CARBS: 9.2G | PROTEIN: 5.3G.

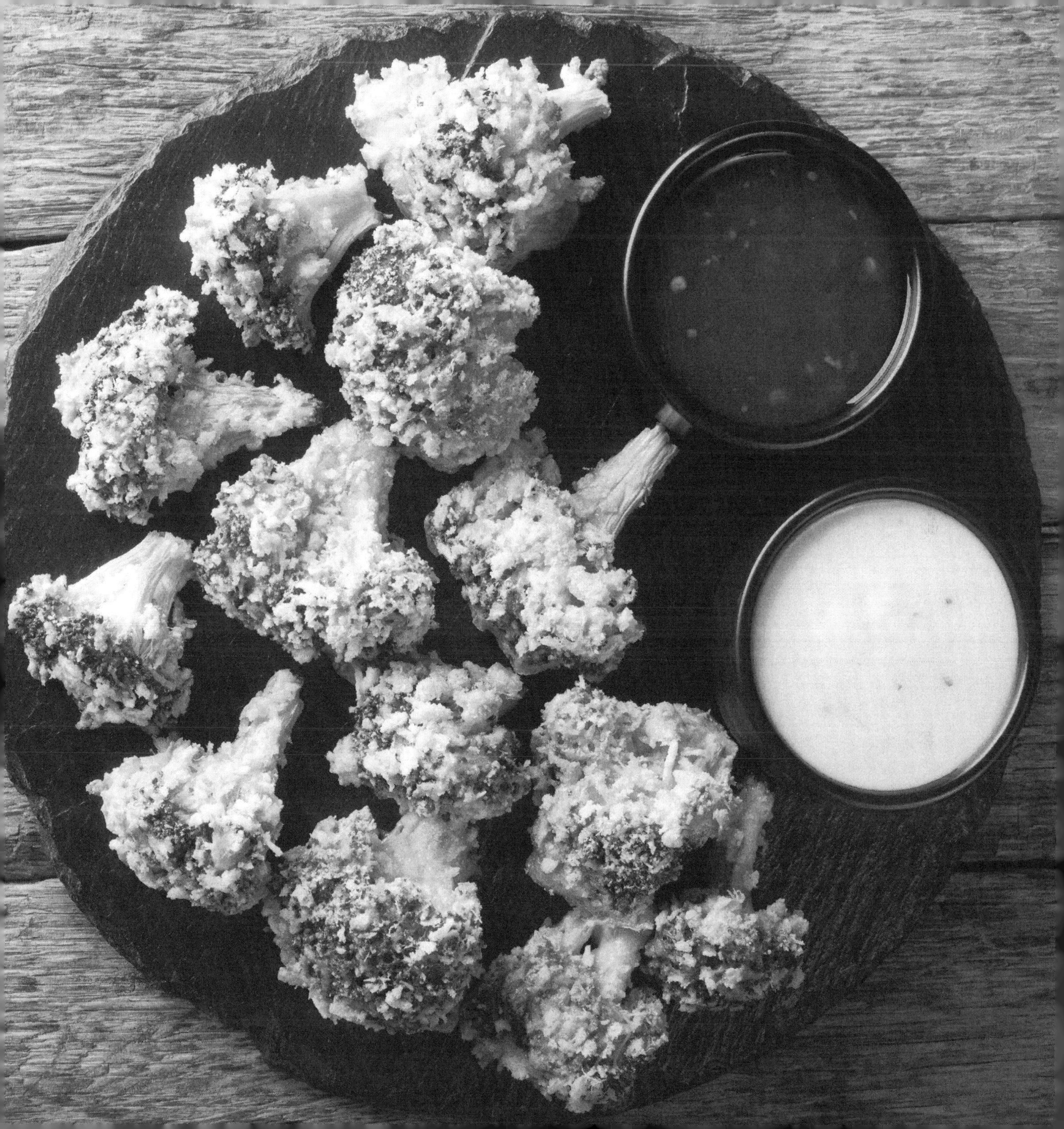

Tasty Oven Cooked Asparagus

Asparagus is such a luxurious vegetable, with it's amazing nutty flavor. By wrapping it in bacon, you get an amazing treat of a side dish!

Servings: 6   Prep Time: 10 Minutes   Cook Time: 20 to 25 Minutes

Ingredients

- 24 asparagus stalks, trimmed
- 1 teaspoon olive oil
- Garlic salt
- Black pepper
- 12 slices bacon

Directions

1. Preheat the oven to 400°F, prepare a deep-sided oven tray with a grill rack.
2. Put the asparagus stalks on a board, chop off the woody ends. Then drizzle with the olive oil and season with the garlic salt and black pepper.
3. Next, cut the bacon slices lengthwise to make long narrow strips.
4. Wrap one bacon strip tightly around each asparagus stalk then place on the grill rack.
5. Bake in the oven for 10 minutes, turn and bake for a further 10 - 15 minutes until the bacon is crispy.
6. Serve immediately.

NUTRITIONAL INFO: CALORIES: 222 | SODIUM: 879MG | DIETARY FIBER: 1G
TOTAL FAT: 16.7G | TOTAL CARBS: 2.4G | PROTEIN: 15.1G.

Parmesan Roasted Cauliflower

Cauliflower and cheese are a classic flavor combination, and this recipe is an easy, healthy way to enjoy them together.

Servings: 4   Prep Time: 5 Minutes   Cook Time: 25 Minutes

Ingredients

1 head cauliflower, cut into florets

3 cloves garlic, minced

1/4 cup olive oil

2 tablespoons lemon juice

1/2 teaspoon salt

1/4 teaspoon black pepper

2 tablespoons parmesan cheese, grated

Directions

1. Preheat the oven to 450°F.
2. In a large bowl, combine the cauliflower florets and garlic.
3. Drizzle over the olive oil and lemon juice. Then season with the salt and pepper. Stir well to combine all the ingredients.
4. Tip onto a large baking sheet and spread into a single even layer.
5. Roast for 25 minutes, giving it a stir after 15 minutes to ensure it is cooked all over.
6. Remove from the oven and sprinkle with the grated parmesan cheese. Serve and enjoy.

NUTRITIONAL INFO: CALORIES: 170 | SODIUM: 375MG | DIETARY FIBER: 3G
TOTAL FAT: 15G | TOTAL CARBS: 9G | PROTEIN: 4G.

Cauliflower Salad

Instead of making a potato salad why not try making a cauliflower salad? This recipe is loaded with flavor and is low in carbs.

Servings: 4   Prep Time: 5 Minutes   Cook Time: 10 Minutes

Ingredients

1 lb. cauliflower

1/3 cup mayonnaise

1 tablespoon olive oil

2 tablespoons white vinegar

1 tablespoon Dijon mustard

1 teaspoon garlic powder

1/4 teaspoon paprika

1/4 teaspoon celery salt

1/4 teaspoon sea salt

1/4 teaspoon pepper

1/4 cup red onion, finely sliced

2 eggs, hard boiled and chopped

1/4 cup scallions, chopped

Directions

1. Steam the cauliflower for 10 minutes until tender, set to one side and allow to cool.

2. Next, in a large bowl whisk the mayonnaise, olive oil, vinegar and mustard together. Then add in the garlic powder, paprika, both salts and the pepper. Whisk again until well combined. Taste to see if it needs more seasoning.

3. Stir in the cauliflower along with the onion, chopped eggs and the scallions.

4. Place in the refrigerator and chill for 30 minutes before serving.

NUTRITIONAL INFO: CALORIES: 227 | SODIUM: 518MG | DIETARY FIBER: 2G
TOTAL FAT: 20G | TOTAL CARBS: 7G | PROTEIN: 5G.

Easy Glazed Carrots

With this simple recipe, say goodbye to picky eaters and hello to kids who ask for more!

Servings: 4   Prep Time: 5 Minutes   Cook Time: 10 Minutes

Ingredients

1 lb. baby carrots
1 tablespoon butter
1 tablespoon honey
1 tablespoon Italian herb mix
Salt and black pepper to taste

Directions

1. Cook the carrots in a small amount of water in a medium sized saucepan for 8 to 10 minutes. Once the carrots are cooked but still a little crisp drain off the water.
2. Add in the butter, honey, and Italian herb mix to the pan. Cook for a further minute over a low heat until the butter is melted, stir to combine.
3. Season with salt and pepper to taste.
4. Serve and enjoy!

NUTRITIONAL INFO: CALORIES: 86 | SODIUM: 319MG | DIETARY FIBER: 3.3G
TOTAL FAT: 3G | TOTAL CARBS: 14.7G | PROTEIN: 0.8G.

Zucchini and Baguette Crouton Salad

The crunchy croutons along with the baked zucchini and fresh tomatoes make for a texture and color sensation! This dish is a great side salad or perfect for a light lunch on its own.

Servings: 14 Cups   Prep Time: 20 Minutes   Cook Time: 40 Minutes

Ingredients

- 3 medium zucchinis, thinly sliced
- 1/4 cup olive oil
- 1 large baguette, cubed to crouton size
- 1-1/2 cups cherry tomatoes, halved
- 1 green pepper, chopped
- 1/2 red onion, thinly sliced
- 1/4 cup balsamic vinegar
- 1 teaspoon jarred roasted minced garlic
- 1 teaspoon Italian seasoning
- 1/2 teaspoon crushed red pepper flakes
- 1 teaspoon salt
- 1/2 teaspoon ground pepper
- 1-1/2 cups fresh mozzarella cheese pearls

Directions

1. Preheat the oven to 400°F.
2. Place the sliced zucchini on a large ovenproof baking tray. Drizzle with 1 tablespoon of the olive oil. Bake in the oven for 25 - 30 minutes turning halfway through. The zucchini is cooked when it is tender and lightly browned. Remove from the oven and set aside to cool.
3. While the zucchini is cooking, make the croutons. Take a large bowl, add the baguette cubes and toss with 1 tablespoon of the olive oil. Place on a baking sheet. Bake in the oven for 12 - 14 minutes until lightly browned.
4. Once the zucchini is cooled, mix with the croutons, tomatoes, green pepper and red onion in a large serving bowl.
5. Make the dressing by mixing together the vinegar, garlic, chili and the rest of the oil in a small bowl. Season with the salt and pepper, whisk well.
6. Drizzle the dressing over zucchini and crouton mixture then toss gently to combine. Add the mozzarella pearls and stir well then serve immediately.

NUTRITIONAL INFO: CALORIES: 152 | SODIUM: 301MG | DIETARY FIBER: 1G
TOTAL FAT: 8G | TOTAL CARBS: 16G | PROTEIN: 5G.

Italian Baked Sweet Potato

Try serving this delicious sweet potato side with sausages - that mix of salt and sweet is a real winner!

Servings: 6   Prep Time: 10 Minutes   Cook Time: 20 Minutes

Ingredients

2 teaspoons garlic, minced

1 tablespoon olive oil

2 tablespoons butter, melted

1/2 teaspoon garlic salt

4 tablespoons parmesan cheese, grated

1/2 teaspoon Italian seasoning

2 sweet potatoes, peeled and cubed

Directions

1. Preheat the oven to 400°F. Line a baking tray with aluminum foil.
2. In a large bowl, mix together the garlic, oil, butter, salt, parmesan cheese and Italian seasoning.
3. Add in the cubes of sweet potatoes and mix until all the potato is well coated in the butter mixture.
4. Transfer to the prepared baking tray and spread the potato out evenly.
5. Bake in the oven for approximately 20 minutes until cooked through and nicely browned.
6. Serve immediately.

NUTRITIONAL INFO: CALORIES: 647 | SODIUM: 815MG | DIETARY FIBER: 8.5G
TOTAL FAT: 42G | TOTAL CARBS: 55G | PROTEIN: 12G.

Sweet and Buttery Butternut Squash

Who can resist this beautifully caramelized squash? Sweet and sticky, this dish is a yummy treat.

Servings: 6   Prep Time: 10 Minutes   Cook Time: 30 Minutes

Ingredients

- 1 medium butternut squash, peeled, deseeded and cubed
- 3 tablespoons butter melted
- 2 tablespoons brown sugar
- 1 teaspoon cinnamon
- 1/2 teaspoon salt
- 1/4 teaspoon pepper

Directions

1. Preheat the oven to 400°F. Line a baking tray with aluminum foil.
2. Spread the prepared butternut squash cubes over the baking tray.
3. Melt the butter in a small saucepan, once melted mix in the brown sugar, cinnamon, salt, and pepper. Stir well until the sugar has dissolved.
4. Pour the mixture over the squash, then give the squash a quick toss to ensure every cube is nicely coated with the butter mixture.
5. Bake in the oven for 30 minutes, turning halfway through to ensure evenly cooked.
6. Serve immediately.

NUTRITIONAL INFO: CALORIES: 131 | SODIUM: 235MG | DIETARY FIBER: 3G
TOTAL FAT: 1G | TOTAL CARBS: 20G | PROTEIN: 1.2G.

Roast Mixed Veggies

This dish is full of color and different textures and is great served straight from the oven or at room temperature.

Servings: 6   Prep Time: 15 Minutes   Cook Time: 40 Minutes

Ingredients

1 1/2 small purple cauliflower heads, cut into florets

1 1/2 small yellow cauliflower heads, cut into florets

6 cups butternut squash, peeled and diced

3 cups mushrooms, sliced

4 1/2 tablespoons extra-virgin olive oil

3 teaspoons salt

Ground black pepper

2 tablespoons flat-leaf parsley, finely chopped

Directions

1. Preheat the oven to 450°F. Prepare a large baking tray by spraying with non-stick spray.
2. Place the cauliflower, butternut squash and mushrooms on the prepared baking tray.
3. Drizzle with the olive oil then season with 2 teaspoons of salt and plenty of black pepper.
4. Toss the vegetables to make sure they are all coated in oil and seasoning.
5. Bake in the oven for 20 minutes, remove and toss again, then bake for a further 20 minutes until the veggies are fully cooked and nicely browned.
6. Sprinkle with the parsley and remaining salt, serve immediately.

NUTRITIONAL INFO: CALORIES: 172 | SODIUM: 1184MG | DIETARY FIBER: 4.3G
TOTAL FAT: 10.8G | TOTAL CARBS: 19.8G | PROTEIN: 3.6G.

Mini Stuffed Tomatoes

Fresh and creamy, these delicious little tomato bites are a super little side or snack.

Servings: 24   **Prep Time: 45 minutes plus 2 hours chilling time**   **Cook Time: No-cooking**

Ingredients

24 cherry tomatoes

1 (3 ounce) packet soft cream cheese

2 tablespoons mayonnaise

1/4 cup cucumber, finely chopped and seeds removed

1 tablespoon spring onions, finely chopped

2 teaspoons fresh dill, chopped

Directions

1. Carefully cut off the leafy part of each tomato.
2. Then, using a teaspoon scoop out the middle of each tomato. Place on kitchen paper the wrong way up to let any excess liquid drip out.
3. Mix the cream cheese and mayonnaise together in a bowl, then add in the cucumber, onions and dill, give the mixture a good stir.
4. Next fill the tomatoes with the cheese mixture, then refrigerate for minimum 2 hours before serving.

NUTRITIONAL INFO: CALORIES: 40 | SODIUM: 25MG | DIETARY FIBER: 1.5G
TOTAL FAT: 1.9G | TOTAL CARBS: 5.3G | PROTEIN: 1.4G.

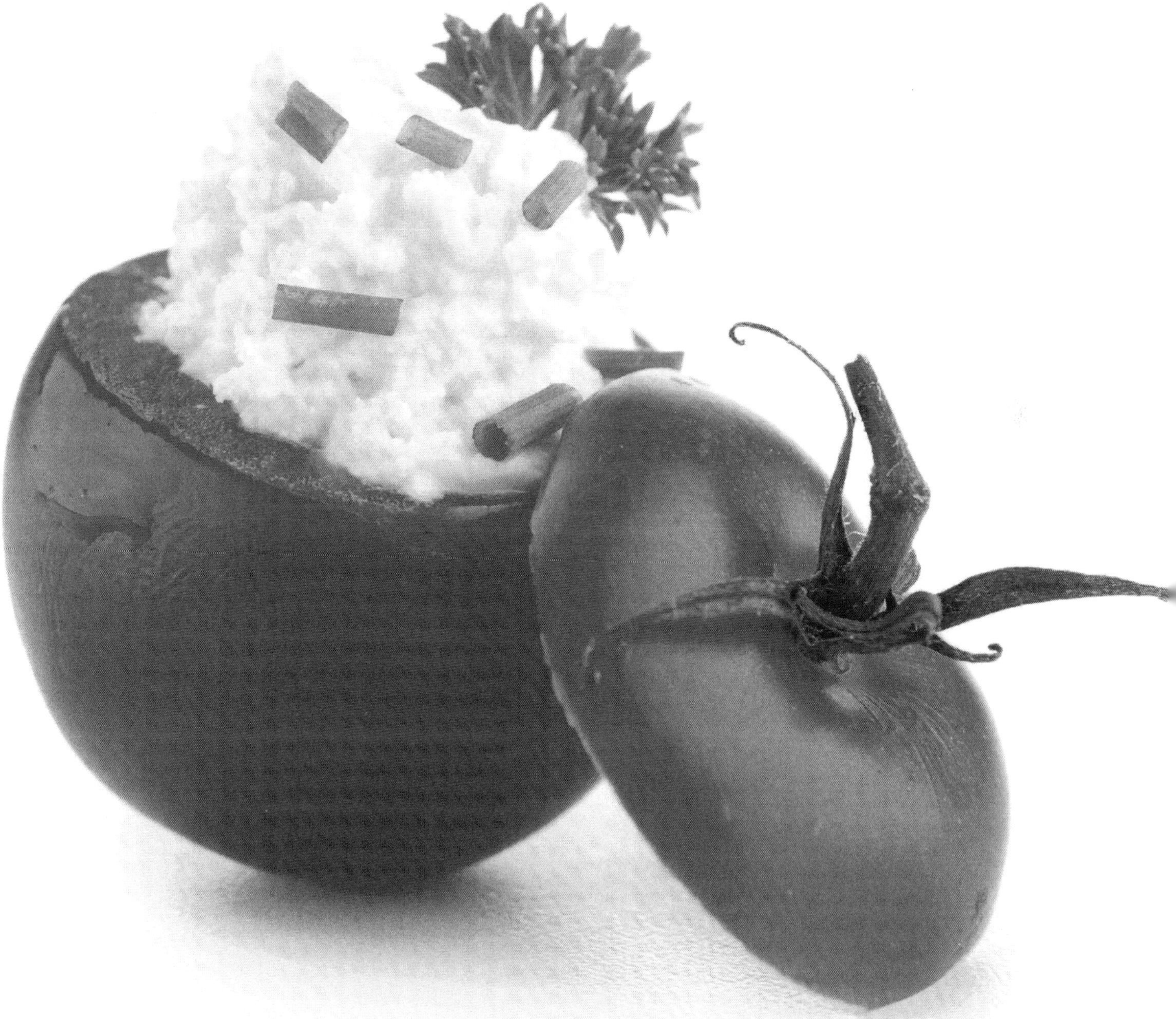

Butternut Squash Patties

These patties are delicious served with sour cream or another topping of your choice!

Servings: 12 Patties   Prep Time: 10 Minutes   Cook Time: 20 Minutes

Ingredients

3 cups butternut squash, peeled and grated
1/2 cup white onion, grated
2 large eggs
1/4 cup whole wheat flour
1/2 teaspoon salt

Directions

1. Preheat the oven to 450°F then warm a baking tray in the oven.
2. In a large bowl, place the grated squash and onion, mix well. Using a potato ricer, put a little squash and onion mixture at a time in the ricer and squeeze well to remove any excess liquid.
3. Once all the excess liquid is removed, add the eggs, flour, and salt to the squash and onions. Mix well until all the ingredients are well combined.
4. Remove the warmed baking tray from the oven and spray with non stick spray.
5. Place scoops of the squash mixture evenly spaced out onto the tray then flatten down. You should end up with 12 patties 3 inches in width.
6. Bake in the oven for 20 minutes, turning halfway. Bake until crispy.
7. Serve warm and enjoy!

NUTRITIONAL INFO: CALORIES: 39 | SODIUM: 110MG | DIETARY FIBER: 6.6G
TOTAL FAT: 0.9G | TOTAL CARBS: 6.6G | PROTEIN: 1.7G.

Quinoa and Herb Salad

Packed full of veggies, this dish is super healthy and full of flavor. Leftovers can be stored in the fridge and are perfect as a lunchbox filler.

Servings: 8   Prep Time: 10 Minutes   Cook Time: 20 Minutes

Ingredients

1 carrot, finely sliced

1 cucumber, chopped

1 cup mixed tomatoes, sliced

1 cup walnuts, toasted

1/2 cup parsley, chopped

1/2 cup mint, chopped

1/2 cup coriander, chopped

1/4 cup chives, chopped

3 spring onions, chopped

1 cup quinoa

FOR THE DRESSING:

1/4 cup (60ml) extra virgin olive oil

2 teaspoons honey

2 garlic cloves, finely chopped

Zest of one orange

Directions

1. Start by preparing all the vegetables and herbs, once chopped, place in a large serving bowl.
2. Next cook the quinoa: Place the quinoa in a saucepan, pour over two cups of water, then bring to the boil. Once boiling, cover and simmer for 10 minutes. Drain and set to one side to cool.
3. Make the dressing by placing the oil, honey, garlic and orange zest into a jar, put on the lid and give it a really good shake till all the ingredients are well combined.
4. Once the quinoa has cooled, pour into the bowl with the vegetables and mix everything together.
5. Finally, pour the dressing on the salad, then toss to combine. Add a little seasoning if required. Serve and enjoy!

NUTRITIONAL INFO: CALORIES: 255 | SODIUM: 14MG | DIETARY FIBER: 4G
TOTAL FAT: 17G | TOTAL CARBS: 21.1G | PROTEIN: 7.8G

Eggplant No-fry Fries

A healthy twist on a fry! This is a great way to get little ones to try different veggies.

Servings: 4   Prep Time: 10 Minutes   Cook Time: 35 - 45 Minutes

Ingredients

1 eggplant
1 tablespoon olive oil
2 teaspoons maple syrup
1 teaspoon sea salt
1/2 teaspoon ground black pepper
1 teaspoon smoked paprika
1 cup almond flour

Directions

1. Preheat the oven to 400°F and prepare a baking sheet with parchment paper.
2. Slice the eggplant into slim fry-like wedges.
3. Place the wedges in a bowl and pour over the olive oil and maple syrup. Then season with the salt and pepper. Next sprinkle over the paprika. Give the bowl a good shake to make sure the wedges are nicely coated.
4. Put the almond flour in a separate bowl. Then add in a few wedges at a time, roll them in the flour until they are well coated then place on the prepared baking sheet, ensuring they are well spaced apart.
5. Bake in the oven for 35 - 45 minutes until crisp and golden brown.
6. Serve with a dip of your choice and enjoy!

NUTRITIONAL INFO: CALORIES: 214 | SODIUM: 605MG | DIETARY FIBER: 7G
TOTAL FAT: 14G | TOTAL CARBS: 17G | PROTEIN: 9G.

Simple Slaw

This is a lovely simple recipe for coleslaw which kids will love. If you're feeling adventurous you can throw in some nuts, seeds or even raisins.

Servings: 12   Prep Time: 20 Minutes   Cook Time: None

Ingredients

- 3/4 green cabbage, shredded
- 1/4 red cabbage, shredded
- 3 medium carrots, grated
- 1 cup mayonnaise
- 2 tablespoons apple cider vinegar
- 1 tablespoon honey
- 1 teaspoon celery seeds
- 1/4 teaspoon salt
- 1/4 teaspoon black pepper

Directions

1. Prepare the vegetables, then place both cabbages and the grated carrot in a bowl.
2. Next, in a separate bowl make the dressing: Whisk together the mayonnaise, vinegar, honey, celery seeds and seasoning.
3. Gradually add a little dressing at a time to the cabbage mixture while continually mixing to ensure the cabbage and carrots are well coated.
4. Either serve immediately or store in the refrigerator until ready to eat.

NUTRITIONAL INFO: CALORIES: 159 | SODIUM: 193MG | DIETARY FIBER: 2G
TOTAL FAT: 14G | CARBS: 8G | PROTEIN: 1G.

Stuffed Baby Portobellos

These mushrooms are a meal in themselves and, are mouth-wateringly delicious! Skip the breadcrumbs to make this recipe gluten free.

Servings: 12 Mushrooms   **Prep Time: 15 Minutes**   **Cook Time: 15 - 20 Minutes**

Ingredients

12 medium-large baby portobellos mushrooms.

2 cloves garlic

1 tablespoon butter

3 cups fresh baby spinach

4 ounces cream cheese

1/4 teaspoon dried basil

1/4 teaspoon salt

1/8 teaspoon black pepper

1/8 teaspoon crushed red pepper flakes

1/4 cup parmesan cheese, grated

2 tablespoons panko breadcrumbs

2 tablespoons parmesan cheese, grated

Directions

1. Preheat the oven to 375°F and prepare a baking sheet with parchment paper.
2. Prepare the mushrooms: Wash, dry and remove the stems. Put the stems aside for the next step. Then place the mushrooms top side down on the baking sheet.
3. Put the stems and garlic on a chopping board and finely chop them together.
4. Next, take a large frying pan, add the butter and melt over a medium to high heat. Then add the finely chopped mushrooms and garlic, and sauté for 3 minutes.
5. Add in the spinach to the pan and fry until wilted. Then put in the cream cheese, basil, seasoning and red pepper flakes. Mix round and cook until the cream cheese has melted.
6. Stir in 1/4 cup grated parmesan cheese then remove from heat.
7. Mix the breadcrumbs and 2 tablespoons grated parmesan in a small bowl.
8. Fill each mushroom with a spoonful of the spinach mixture, then sprinkle with a little of the breadcrumb mix.
9. Bake in the oven for 15 to 20 minutes until the mushrooms are soft and the filling is melted.
10. Serve and enjoy!

NUTRITIONAL INFO: CALORIES: 159 | SODIUM: 193MG | DIETARY FIBER: 2G
TOTAL FAT: 14G | TOTAL CARBS: 8G | PROTEIN: 1G.

Crispy Greens

Steaming or boiling beans can make them rubbery and a bit tasteless. So, here's a great way to keep both the texture and flavor perfect. If you don't have fresh green beans, then use frozen beans, just defrost before you start.

Servings: 4   Prep Time: 20 Minutes   Cook Time: 20 Minutes

Ingredients

- 3 cups fresh green beans, washed and trimmed
- 2 eggs, beaten
- 1 cup panko breadcrumbs
- 1/2 teaspoon garlic powder
- 1/2 teaspoon salt
- 1/2 teaspoon black pepper

Directions

1. Preheat the oven to 425°F and spray a baking tray with non-stick spray.
2. Prepare the green beans.
3. Beat the eggs together in a bowl.
4. In a separate bowl, mix the breadcrumbs, garlic powder and seasoning together.
5. One at a time, dip the green beans into the egg mixture, then roll in the breadcrumbs and then place on the baking tray.
6. Make sure the beans are well spaced out on the tray, then bake in the oven for 10-15 minutes until crispy and golden brown.
7. Serve immediately.

NUTRITIONAL INFO: CALORIES: 126 | SODIUM: 438MG | DIETARY FIBER: 4G
TOTAL FAT: 3G | TOTAL CARBS: 19G | PROTEIN: 7G.

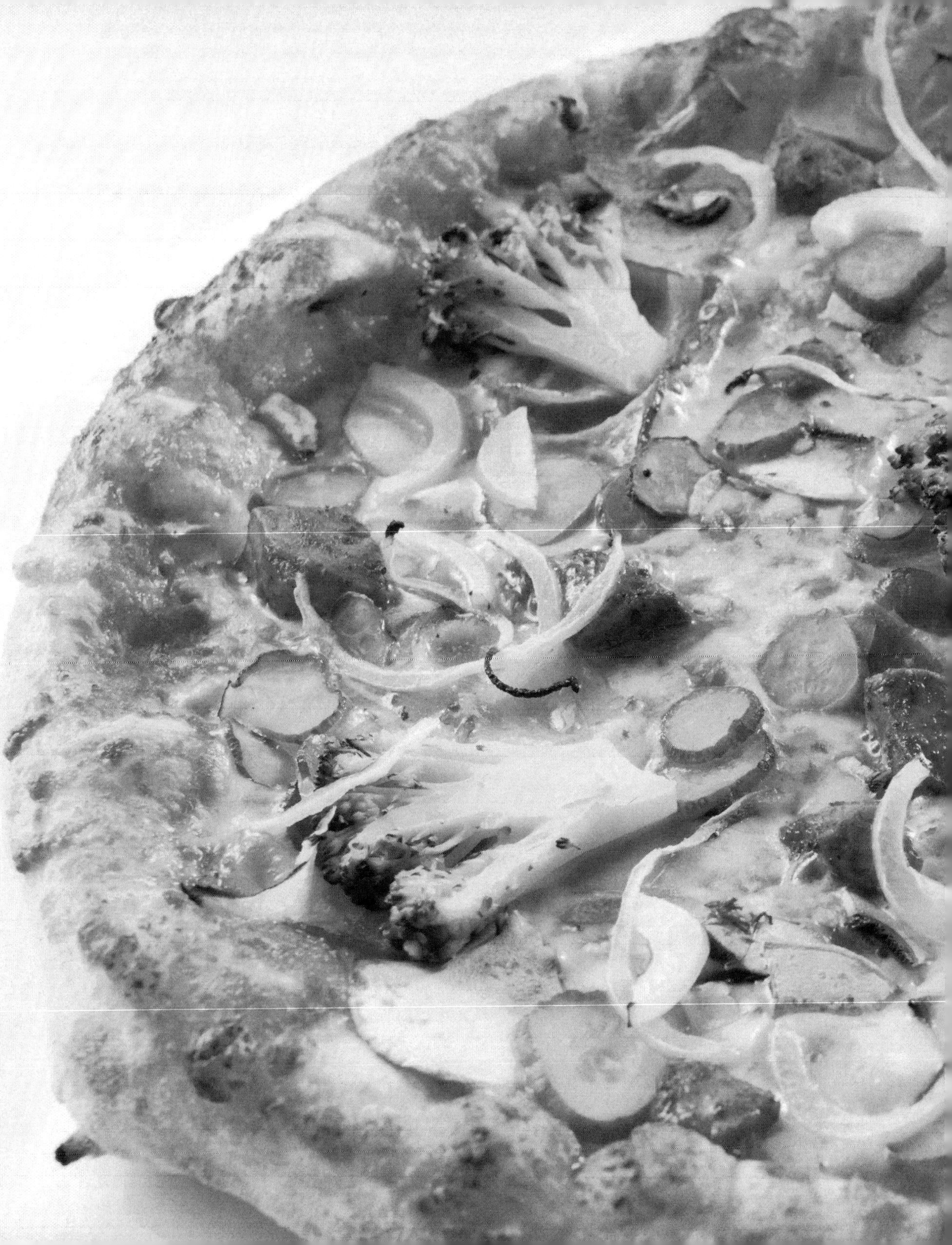

CHAPTER 9
Dinner

Meat and Veggie Balls

These meat and veggie balls are delicious served either with a tomato sauce and pasta or with a creamy sauce and potatoes.

Servings: 18 Meatballs   **Prep Time:** 15 Minutes   **Cook Time:** 20 - 25 Minutes

Ingredients

- 1 lb. ground beef
- 3/4 teaspoon salt
- 1/4 teaspoon pepper
- 1 1/2 teaspoons Italian seasoning
- 2 tablespoons flax meal
- 1 1/2 cups broccoli florets
- 1 large carrot, peeled and roughly chopped
- 1 1/2 cups baby spinach
- 2 stalks green onions
- 1 clove garlic

Directions

1. Preheat the oven to 400°F and prepare a large baking sheet with non-stick spray.
2. In a large bowl mix the beef, seasoning and flax meal.
3. Use a food processor to finely chop the broccoli, carrots, baby spinach, green onions and garlic together.
4. Add the finely chopped vegetables to the meat mixture, then use your hands to combine the ingredients really well.
5. Next roll the mixture into small balls, approximately the size of a golf ball, being careful not to overwork the mixture.
6. Layout the meatballs on the baking sheet, leaving a little space in between each ball.
7. Bake in the oven for 20 to 25 minutes until brown and cooked through.

NUTRITIONAL INFO: CALORIES: 74 | SODIUM: 122MG | DIETARY FIBER: 4G
TOTAL FAT: 5G | TOTAL CARBS: 1G | PROTEIN: 5G.

Individual Shepherd's Pies

There are so many variations of this classic British dish, and this one is a real winner with the crescent dough forming a beautiful base. Serve with a side of Roasted Broccoli.

Servings: 12   Prep Time: 25 Minutes   Cook Time: 40 Minutes

Ingredients

2 large potatoes
1 onion, finely chopped
1/2 lb. lean ground beef
1 teaspoon steak seasoning
1 tablespoon tomato ketchup
1 teaspoon Worcestershire sauce
1/3 cup mixed frozen vegetables
3 tablespoons single cream
1 (8 ounce) can crescent dough sheet

Directions

1. Preheat the oven to 375°F. Prepare a muffin tin by spraying a little non-stick spray in each cup.
2. Prepare the potatoes: Peel and cut each one into 4, then boil in lightly salted water for 15 minutes until soft.
3. Meanwhile, heat a little olive oil in a large frying pan, add the onion and sauté for 3 minutes until softened.
4. Add the ground beef and steak seasoning, then brown the meat on a medium high heat, all the time stirring to break up the meat.
5. Add in the ketchup, Worcestershire sauce, frozen vegetables and seasoning. Continue to cook for a further 5 minutes. Remove from heat.
6. The potatoes should now be cooked and ready to drain. Once drained return to the pan, add the cream and a little seasoning, and mash well.
7. Next, lightly flour the work surface, unroll the crescent dough and work into a 12 x 9-inch rectangle.
8. Cut the dough into 12 equally sized squares, then press one square into each muffin cup so that it covers the bottom and the sides of the cup.
9. Next, put 2 tablespoons of the beef into each cup then a spoonful of mashed potato on top.
10. Bake in the oven for 15 - 20 minutes until golden brown.
11. Carefully remove each mini pie from the tin and serve.

NUTRITIONAL INFO: CALORIES: 169 | SODIUM: 237MG | DIETARY FIBER: 2.5G
TOTAL FAT: 5G | TOTAL CARBS: 22.1G | PROTEIN: 8.4G.

Sweetcorn Patties

These crispy, delicious little patties are colorful and so tasty. They can either be eaten the same day or stored in the fridge and eaten the next day.

Servings: 8 Patties   Prep Time: 10 Minutes   Cook Time: 5 - 10 Minutes

Ingredients

3/4 cups sweetcorn

8 piccolo cherry tomatoes, roughly chopped

1 clove garlic, crushed

2 tablespoons basil, chopped

1 tablespoon sweet chili sauce

1/3 cup plain flour

1 teaspoon baking powder

1/4 cup parmesan cheese, grated

1 egg, beaten

Directions

1. Using a food processor, whizz the sweetcorn until it forms a paste. Then transfer to a bowl.
2. Add the tomatoes, garlic, basil and sweet chili sauce. Mix well.
3. Next add the flour, baking powder, parmesan cheese and egg, stir until well combined.
4. Heat a tablespoon of olive oil in a frying pan. Then use an ice-cream scoop to scoop out balls of the mixture, place directly into the pan then flatten them out to make a patty.
5. Fry on each side for 3 to 4 minutes until golden.
6. Serve with a side salad and enjoy!

NUTRITIONAL INFO: CALORIES: 71 | SODIUM: 83MG | DIETARY FIBER: 0.9G
TOTAL FAT: 2.4G | TOTAL CARBS: 8.6G | PROTEIN: 4.5G.

Easy Vegetarian Pizza

Using crescent dough is a great pizza shortcut. Topped with loads of fresh veggies this pizza is both delicious and nutritious!

Servings: 16 Servings   **Prep Time:** 15 Minutes   **Cook Time:** 20 Minutes

Ingredients

2 (8 ounce) cans crescent dough

2 (8 ounce) packets cream cheese, softened

1 cup mayonnaise

1 packet dry ranch dressing mix

1 cup broccoli, cut into florets

1 cup cauliflower, cut into florets

1 cup carrots, grated

1 cup cheddar cheese, grated

OPTIONAL:

1/4 cup each bell pepper, tomato, or black olives, chopped

Directions

1. Preheat the oven to 375°F and line a large baking sheet with parchment paper.
2. Roll out both packages of the crescent dough onto the baking sheet to make one large rectangular base.
3. Bake in the oven according to the instructions on the can. Once cooked, allow to cool fully.
4. While the base cools, mix the cream cheese, mayonnaise and ranch dressing together in a bowl. Then place in the refrigerator to chill.
5. Once the base is fully cooled, spread with the cream cheese mixture.
6. Next, spread the chopped vegetables evenly over the top. Then sprinkle over a layer of cheese.
7. Finish off with any of the optional vegetables that you choose to use.
8. Chill briefly before slicing and serving.

NUTRITIONAL INFO: CALORIES: 234 | SODIUM: 496MG | DIETARY FIBER: 1G
TOTAL FAT: 19G | TOTAL CARBS: 14G | PROTEIN: 3G.

Zucchini Risotto

Take your time to cook the rice slowly to ensure you get that glossy, creamy rice that is super delicious.

Servings: 4 People   **Prep Time: 20 Minutes**   **Cook Time: 1 hour**

Ingredients

6 cups hot vegetable stock
3 tablespoons butter
1 onion, chopped
2 spring onions, chopped
1 cup risotto rice
Salt and freshly ground black pepper
1 tablespoon olive oil
3 medium zucchinis, cubed
Small bunch fresh parsley, chopped
1/3 cup parmesan cheese, grated

Directions

1. Pour 5 cups of the hot stock into a saucepan and keep on a low heat so it stays hot but not boiling.
2. In a large pan, melt 1 tablespoon of butter, then add the onion and spring onion and fry for 2 minutes over a medium heat until soft.
3. Add in the rice, make sure to keep stirring while cooking for a further 2 minutes.
4. Once the rice appears translucent, pour in the last cup of stock, again stirring all the time, simmer until all the liquid has been absorbed.
5. Season with salt and pepper.
6. Next, add a ladleful of stock at a time to the rice, continue to simmer and stir until all the liquid has been absorbed and the rice is cooked - it should be soft but have a slight bite. Take your time over this as you don't want the rice to cook too quickly.
7. Check the seasoning and add in a little more if required.
8. In a separate frying pan, melt 1 tablespoon butter then add the olive oil. Add in the zucchini and gently fry until softened and browned, approximately 5 minutes.
9. Gently stir the cooked zucchini into the rice, then add the parsley, parmesan cheese and a tablespoon of butter, give everything a really good stir to ensure it is fully combined.
10. Serve and enjoy!

NUTRITIONAL INFO: CALORIES: 183 | SODIUM: 480MG | DIETARY FIBER: 2.4G
TOTAL FAT: 9.7G | TOTAL CARBS: 21G | PROTEIN: 3.8G.

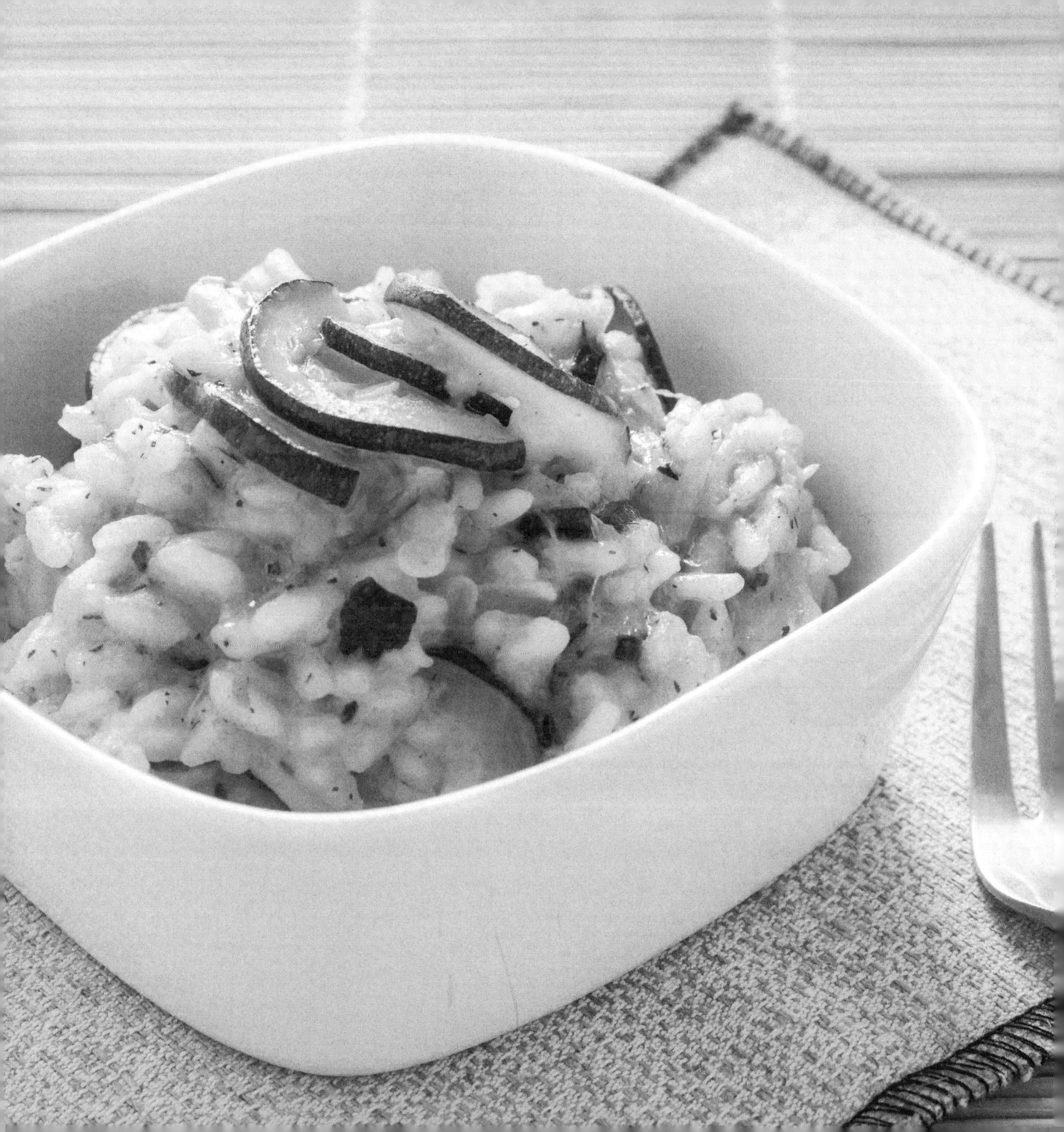

Cauliflower Cheese Fritters

Filling and satisfying, these healthy fritters are great served with a dollop of sour cream.

Servings: 16   Prep Time: 10 Min   Cook Time: 20 Min

Ingredients

- 1 lb. cauliflower, cut into florets
- 2 eggs, beaten
- 1/2 cup Parmesan cheese
- 2/3 cup Panko breadcrumbs
- 1/2 teaspoon garlic powder
- 1 tablespoon parsley, chopped
- 1/2 teaspoon salt
- 1/4 teaspoon black pepper
- 2 ounces Mozzarella cheese, cubed

Directions

1. Preheat the oven to 400°F, line a baking tray with parchment paper.
2. Steam the cauliflower until softened. Drain, then leave in the colander to air dry for a few minutes. Transfer to a bowl, then mash until it is a smooth consistency.
3. Add in the beaten eggs, Parmesan cheese, breadcrumbs, garlic powder, parsley and seasoning, and mix well. The mixture should not be too wet or too dry.
4. Use an ice-cream scoop to scoop out balls of the mixture, place on the baking tray then push a cube of Mozzarella cheese into the middle of each ball. Finally, using the back of a spoon flatten down slightly to make a patty shape.
5. Bake in the oven for 20 minutes, turning half way through, the patties should be golden brown once cooked.
6. Serve and enjoy!

NUTRITIONAL INFO: CALORIES: 48 | SODIUM: 179MG | DIETARY FIBER: 4G
TOTAL FAT: 2G | TOTAL CARBS: 3G | PROTEIN: 3G.

Yummy Fishy Pie

Fish is a great source of protein, combined with potatoes and cheese sauce makes for an irresistible dish. Serve with a side of Crispy Greens.

Servings: 4   Prep Time: 20 Minutes   Cook Time: 45 Minutes

Ingredients

2 lbs. potatoes (unpeeled)

6 ounces salmon fillets (skin on)

6 ounces smoked haddock fillets (skin on)

2 tablespoons cheddar cheese, grated

FOR THE SAUCE:

2 tablespoons butter

2 tablespoons plain flour

1-pint whole milk

1/2 cup cheddar cheese, grated

1 cup spinach

Directions

1. Preheat the oven to 350°F.
2. Leave the skins on the potatoes, cut into quarters, then boil in slightly salted water for approximately 20 minutes until softened but still a little firm. Drain and allow to air dry in a colander.
3. Keeping the skin on the fish, place in an ovenproof dish and bake in the oven for 10 minutes. Take out of the oven, carefully remove the skins and flake the fish, set to one side.
4. Next, make the cheese sauce: gently melt the butter in a saucepan, add the flour and stir, continue to cook for 1 minute.
5. Remove the saucepan from the heat and add a little milk, stirring quickly. When you have a smooth paste, add a little more milk and return to the heat, keep stirring to prevent lumps forming whilst adding a little milk at a time until all the milk is used, and you have a smooth thick sauce.
6. Remove from the heat and add the cheese and spinach, give it a good stir so the cheese melts into the sauce and the spinach wilts.
7. Slice the potatoes into 1cm thick slices.
8. Pour the cheese sauce over the fish, then top with the potato slices. Finish with a sprinkling of grated cheese.
9. Bake for 15 to 20 minutes until cooked through and browned on top.
10. Serve immediately.

NUTRITIONAL INFO: CALORIES: 269 | SODIUM: 55MG | DIETARY FIBER: 5.4G
TOTAL FAT: 4.3G | TOTAL CARBS: 35.7G | PROTEIN: 22.8G.

Vegetarian Nuggets

Serve these super-healthy little balls with as many different dipping sauces as you can find to make a fun dinner time tasting game!

Servings: 24 Nuggets   Prep Time: 25 Minutes   Cook Time: 30 Minutes

Ingredients

1 cup split red lentils
2 slices whole grain bread
1/4 cup frozen peas
1/4 cup frozen corn
1 large carrot, grated
1 medium zucchini, grated
1/2 teaspoon sea salt
1/4 teaspoon garlic powder
1/4 teaspoon oregano
1/2 teaspoon paprika

Directions

1. Preheat the oven to 425°F, line a large baking sheet with parchment paper.
2. Put the lentils in a bowl and cover with boiling water, leave to soak for 30 minutes.
3. Place the slices of bread in a food processor and blitz to form breadcrumbs. Then, put the breadcrumbs in a bowl along with the frozen peas and corn, set to one side.
4. Drain the lentils then place in the food processor with the carrot, zucchini and seasonings. Blitz to a paste.
5. Add the lentil mixture into the bowl with the breadcrumbs, peas and corn. Mix really well until everything is well combined.
6. Use your hands to roll the mixture into small balls, about the size of a ping pong ball. Place the balls on the prepared baking sheet.
7. Bake in the oven for 30 mins, turning halfway. Remove from the oven and allow to cool and firm up for 5 minutes before serving.

NUTRITIONAL INFO: CALORIES: 39 | SODIUM: 56MG | DIETARY FIBER: 2.9G
TOTAL FAT: 0.2G | TOTAL CARBS: 7G | PROTEIN: 2.6G.

Patty Towers

Looking for a carb free dinner, then look no further! Serve with salad for a fresh taste.

Servings: 8   Prep Time: 20 Mins   Cook Time: 5 Mins

Ingredients

2 lbs. ground beef
1/2 cup bacon, cooked and crumbled
2 tablespoons dill pickle juice
1 1/2 teaspoons onion powder
1 teaspoon black pepper
1/2 teaspoon salt
6 ounces cheddar cheese, sliced

Directions

1. Preheat the oven to 425°F, line a baking sheet with parchment paper.
2. Put the beef, crumbled bacon, dill juice, onion powder and seasoning in a large bowl. Use your hands to mix well until all the ingredients are well combined.
3. Take tablespoonfuls of the mixture, then roll between your palms into a rough ball, place onto the prepared baking sheet then squash down to make a patty shape.
4. Bake in the oven for 5 minutes on each side or until browned and cooked through.
5. Remove the patties from the baking sheet and place on a dish lined with a paper towel.
6. Make the patty towers by placing a slice of cheese on top of a patty then top with a second patty.
7. Serve with barbeque dipping sauce.

NUTRITIONAL INFO: CALORIES: 363 | SODIUM: 650MG | DIETARY FIBER: 0.1G
TOTAL FAT: 19.1G | TOTAL CARBS: 1G | PROTEIN: 44.2G.

Easy Peasy Chicken on a Stick

Chicken on a stick is the best excuse for eating with your fingers! Serve with Eggplant No-fry Fries to make this tasty dish even more nutritious.

Servings: 4   Prep Time: 45 Minutes   Cook Time: 15 Minutes

Ingredients

EQUIPMENT:

- 4 wooden skewers
- 1 1/2 lbs. chicken breasts, diced
- 2 red peppers, diced
- 2 red onions, diced

FOR THE MARINADE:

- 1/2 cup pineapple juice
- 2 tablespoons soy sauce
- 2 tablespoons olive oil
- 1 tablespoon honey
- 1 teaspoon garlic powder
- 1/2 teaspoon red pepper flakes

Directions

1. Place the wooden skewers in a bowl of cold water and leave to soak for 30 minutes.
2. Mix the chicken, red pepper, and onions together in a bowl.
3. In a separate bowl, place all the marinade ingredients and whisk until fully combined.
4. Pour the marinade over the chicken and vegetables, mix round to ensure everything is well coated then place in the refrigerator for 30 minutes.
5. Skewer the chicken and vegetables - evenly distributing the chicken and vegetables between each skewer.
6. Heat a heavy based grill pan on a medium to high heat.
7. Grill the chicken skewers for 10 to 15 minutes, turning several times while cooking. The chicken is ready when golden brown and fully cooked through.

NUTRITIONAL INFO: CALORIES: 454 | SODIUM: 603MG | DIETARY FIBER: 1.8G
TOTAL FAT: 19.9G | TOTAL CARBS: 16.7G | PROTEIN: 51G.

Mixed Grilled Sandwich

In need of a light, quick dinner? Adding broccoli to this grilled cheese is a perfect way to add some extra nutrients.

Servings: 1   Prep Time: 10 Minutes   Cook Time: 5 Minutes

Ingredients

FOR THE FILLING:

1/3 cup cheddar cheese, grated

2 tablespoons parmesan cheese, grated

1/4 cup ham, finely chopped

6 small broccoli florets, steamed

1/8 teaspoon onion powder

1/8 teaspoon garlic powder

Salt and pepper

2 slices whole wheat bread

1 tablespoon extra-virgin olive oil

Directions

1. Mix all the filling ingredients together in a bowl, stir well to fully combine.
2. Lay a slice of bread on a board, cover with the filling mixture, then top with another slice of bread.
3. Heat 1/2 tablespoon olive oil in a frying pan over a medium heat.
4. Fry the sandwich in the pan for 2 to 3 minutes each side. Add the remaining oil when you turn the sandwich over. Gently press down the sandwich with a spatula whilst it cooks.
5. Cook until golden brown and the cheese has melted.
6. Eat while still warm!

NUTRITIONAL INFO: CALORIES: 540 | SODIUM: 1149MG | DIETARY FIBER: 2.9G
TOTAL FAT: 35.8G | TOTAL CARBS: 30G | PROTEIN: 26.3G.

Indonesian Style Chicken Skewers

Although this recipe requires a lot of different ingredients, it's easy to make, and the result is a true taste sensation! This dish goes great with a side of Simple Slaw.

Servings: 6   Prep Time: 45 Min   Cook Time: 10 Min

Ingredients

EQUIPMENT:

6 wooden skewers

2 lbs. chicken breast cut into 1-inch cubes

FOR THE MARINADE:

1/4 cup dried lemongrass

1/4 yellow onion

4 cloves garlic

1 teaspoon Sriracha

1-inch piece fresh ginger

1/2 teaspoon turmeric

2 tablespoons ground coriander

1 tablespoon cumin

1/4 cup dark soy sauce

2 tablespoons fish sauce

1/3 cup brown sugar

2 tablespoons vegetable oil

FOR THE PEANUT SAUCE:

1 cup smooth peanut butter

1/3 cup lite soy sauce

3 cloves garlic

2 tablespoons sesame oil

1-inch piece fresh ginger

1 teaspoon sriracha

2 limes, juiced and zested

Directions

1. Start by putting the wooden skewers in a bowl of cold water and leave to soak.
2. Next, put the chicken cubes in a large bowl.
3. Then, using a food processor, blend together all the marinade ingredients until you have a smooth paste.
4. Pour the paste over the chicken and stir well. Place in the fridge and leave to marinate for an hour, or longer if you have time.
5. Remove the wooden skewers from the water.
6. Skewer the chicken - dividing equally between each skewer.
7. Heat a heavy based grill pan and cook the chicken skewers on a high heat for 3 minutes on each side until nicely browned.
8. Finally make the peanut sauce by putting all the sauce ingredients into a food processor and blending until you have a smooth paste.
9. Put the cooked chicken skewers on a plate, with the sauce in a small bowl alongside and serve!

NUTRITIONAL INFO: CALORIES: 572 | SODIUM: 1601MG | DIETARY FIBER: 3.6G
TOTAL FAT: 34.9G | TOTAL CARBS: 24.5G | PROTEIN: 44.8G.

Sticky Chicken

Coconut aminos is a great substitute for soy sauce and great for those with food sensitivities.

Servings: 4   Prep Time: 40 Minutes   Cook Time: 15 Minutes

Ingredients

1 1/2 lbs. boneless skinless chicken thighs

1/4 cup honey

1/2 cup coconut aminos

1 garlic clove, crushed

1/4 teaspoon fresh ginger, grated

2 tablespoons oil

2 cups cooked white rice

Directions

1. Start by tenderizing the chicken, pound until it is approximately 1/4 inch thick.
2. Put the honey, coconut aminos, garlic, and ginger in a large bowl and whisk until well combined.
3. Add in the chicken and mix well so that all the chicken is covered in the honey mixture. Place in the refrigerator for at least 30 minutes to marinate.
4. Heat the oil in a large frying pan on a medium high heat, then cook the chicken in batches for 5 minutes on each side. Leave the marinade in the bowl. Once the chicken is fully cooked, transfer to a plate and set to one side.
5. Pour the marinade into the frying pan, bring to the boil then simmer for a couple of minutes to reduce and thicken. Add the chicken back in and give it a good stir.
6. Once the chicken is warmed through remove from the heat and serve with the rice.

NUTRITIONAL INFO: CALORIES: 542 | SODIUM: 77MG | DIETARY FIBER: 1.3G
TOTAL FAT: 9.1G | TOTAL CARBS: 97.7G | PROTEIN: 15G.

Stir Fry Cauliflower Rice

This is the ultimate comfort food; warm, satisfying and healthy to boot.

Servings: 4   Prep Time: 10 Minutes   Cook Time: 10 Minutes

Ingredients

1 large head cauliflower, cut into florets

1 tablespoon sesame oil

1 bunch green onions, chopped, whites separated from greens

1/2 cup frozen peas

1/2 cup carrots, cubed

3 eggs, beaten

1/2 lb. shrimp, thawed, peeled and deveined

FOR THE TAMARI SAUCE:

1/4 cup coconut aminos or soy sauce

1 tablespoon honey

1/2 teaspoon fresh ginger, grated

Pinch red pepper flakes

Directions

1. Using a food processor, add in the cauliflower florets and blitz until it looks similar to rice.
2. Make the Tamari sauce: Put the coconut aminos, honey, ginger and red pepper flakes in a bowl and whisk well, then put to one side.
3. Heat the sesame oil in a large wok on a medium to high heat. Add in the whites of the onions and fry for approximately one minute.
4. Add in the frozen peas and carrots. Continue to cook for a further 2 minutes then push the vegetables over to one side of the wok.
5. Pour in the beaten egg to the empty side of the wok, while it cooks move it around to break it up.
6. Next, add in the shrimp and cook until pink.
7. Add the riced cauliflower to the wok and stir well. Lastly, pour over the Tamari sauce and mix well. Cook for a further 5 minutes until the cauliflower is tender but still has a bit of bite.
8. Plate up and sprinkle over the green onions before serving.

NUTRITIONAL INFO: CALORIES: 249 | SODIUM: 286MG | DIETARY FIBER: 6.8G
TOTAL FAT: 7.9G | TOTAL CARBS: 23.7G | PROTEIN: 22.5G.

Tasty Tofu Stir-Fry

Pick a firm or extra firm tofu to give this dish good texture. Additionally, you can use peanut or coconut oil if you prefer.

Servings: 6   Prep Time: 15 Minutes   Cook Time: 45 Minutes

Ingredients

FOR THE STIR FRY:

2 (14-ounce) packages firm tofu
4 tablespoons toasted sesame oil
4 cups green beans, chopped
1 cup red pepper, diced
1 cup carrots, diced

FOR THE SAUCE:

1/2 cup low-sodium soy sauce
2 tablespoons fresh ginger, grated
4 tablespoons brown sugar
2 tablespoons agave or maple syrup
2 tablespoons cornstarch

TO SERVE:

Rice
Peanut sauce

Directions

1. Preheat the oven to 400°F, line a baking sheet with parchment paper.
2. Remove the tofu from the package, drain, then fold 2 tea-towels around the tofu. Place on a plate then put another plate on top. Add a heavy weight on top of the top plate in order to squeeze out any excess liquid from the tofu. Leave it for 15 minutes, check halfway through and change the towels if they become too wet.
3. Once the tofu has dried out, cut it into cubes (approximately 1 inch in size) then place on the prepared baking sheet and bake in the oven for 30 minutes, until golden brown, making sure to turn halfway through cooking time. Once cooked, set to one side for 30 minutes.
4. Next prepare the sauce, whisk all the ingredients together in a bowl, once well mixed, put to one side.
5. Heat the sesame oil in a large frying pan over a medium to high heat.
6. Add in the beans, peppers and carrots, stir and cook for 6 to 7 minutes until the vegetables are slightly browned and softened.
7. Pour over the sauce and continue to cook until the sauce has thickened and reduced slightly.
8. Add in the tofu and stir well so everything is covered in the sauce. Cook for a further 5 minutes.
9. Serve with the rice and peanut sauce and enjoy!

NUTRITIONAL INFO: CALORIES: 286 | SODIUM: 41MG | DIETARY FIBER: 3.9G
TOTAL FAT: 16.1G | TOTAL CARBS: 26G | PROTEIN: 13.4G.

Citrus Stir Fry

This dish is both sweet and savory, just perfect for little ones! Serve with steamed rice and stir fry vegetables

Servings: 4   Prep Time: 10 Minutes   Cook Time: 20 Minutes

Ingredients

2 oranges, whole

2 cloves garlic, crushed

2 tablespoons soy sauce

1 tablespoon cornstarch

1 tablespoon canola oil

1 1/2 lbs. trimmed boneless sirloin ribeye or flank steak, cut into thin strips

Salt and pepper to taste

3 green onions, sliced

2 oranges, peeled and cut into segments

1 tablespoon sesame seeds

Directions

1. Start by grating the zest from one orange, then juice 2 oranges.
2. Place the zest and juice together in a bowl. Stir in the crushed garlic and soy sauce.
3. Next mix together the cornstarch and a tablespoon of water, then add into the orange mixture.
4. Put a large frying pan over a high heat, add the canola oil, then add the beef in batches and cook for 5 minutes. Season and keep moving the meat around while cooking so it cooks all over. Once all the beef is cooked move to a plate.
5. Pour the orange juice mix into the pan and simmer for around 3 minutes until it starts to thicken.
6. Add the beef back into the pan along with the green onions and orange segments, toss to combine and continue to cook for another 5 minutes.
7. Sprinkle with the sesame seeds and serve with rice.

NUTRITIONAL INFO: CALORIES: 493 | SODIUM: 573MG | DIETARY FIBER: 5.1G
TOTAL FAT: 29.5G | TOTAL CARBS: 25.9G | PROTEIN: 31.9G.

Zesty Fried Chicken

Try serving this dish with Italian Baked Sweet Potato or with Sweet and Buttery Butternut Squash

Servings: 8   Prep Time: 15 Minutes   Cook Time: 15 Minutes

Ingredients

4 large chicken breasts
1 teaspoon salt
1/2 teaspoon ground black pepper
3/4 cups plain flour
3 tablespoons olive oil
3 tablespoons butter
2 cloves garlic, crushed
3/4 cups chicken stock
1 large lemon, zested
4 tablespoons lemon juice

TO GARNISH:

Parsley or basil
Lemon wedges

Directions

1. Slice the chicken breasts lengthwise into long thin strips.
2. Season the chicken strips with salt and pepper.
3. Put the flour in a large shallow sided plate, then add in the chicken, roll each piece around so that it is well coated in flour.
4. Heat 2 teaspoons of oil in a large frying pan over a medium heat.
5. Fry the chicken in batches for 5 minutes on each side, once cooked put on a plate. Add more oil as necessary.
6. Melt a tablespoon of butter in the frying pan, then add the garlic, fry for 30 seconds. Keep moving the garlic around the pan to stop it burning.
7. Add the rest of the butter to the pan, then the chicken stock, lemon zest and the juice. Simmer and stir continuously for 2 to 3 minutes, making sure to scrape along the base and sides of the pan to ensure everything mixes together really well.
8. Put the chicken back into the pan with the sauce and stir to make sure the chicken is fully covered with the sauce. Cook for a couple of minutes, then serve with the garnish.

NUTRITIONAL INFO: CALORIES: 188 | SODIUM: 419MG | DIETARY FIBER: 0.6G
TOTAL FAT: 11G | TOTAL CARBS: 10.2G | PROTEIN: 12.1G.

Spicy Shrimp Wraps

Choose regular, whole wheat or gluten free tortillas to suit your taste. Serve with any extra toppings that your little ones like.

Servings: 10 Tacos   **Prep Time:** 5 Minutes   **Cook Time:** 12 - 15 Minutes

Ingredients

1 lb. uncooked shrimp, thawed, peeled and deveined

1/4 red onion, thinly sliced

1 red pepper, sliced

1 yellow pepper, sliced

2 teaspoons paprika

1 teaspoon chili powder

1/2 teaspoon onion powder

1/2 teaspoon garlic powder

1/2 teaspoon cumin

Salt and pepper, to taste

10 tortillas

1 lime

Directions

1. Preheat the oven to 450°F, and line a baking sheet with aluminum foil.
2. Place the shrimp on the baking sheet along with the onion and peppers.
3. Mix all the spices and seasoning together in a small bowl then sprinkle over the shrimp and veggies, toss to ensure that everything is well coated.
4. Next, stack the tortillas and wrap with aluminum foil.
5. Place both the baking sheet with the shrimp and veggies, and the tortillas in the oven and bake for 8 to 10 minutes.
6. Remove the tortillas from the oven then switch oven setting to broil and continue to cook the shrimp for another 3 minutes until golden.
7. Remove from the oven and squeeze over the lime.
8. Serve by placing some of the shrimp and veggie mixture into each tortilla and add some extra toppings if you would like.

NUTRITIONAL INFO: CALORIES: 122 | SODIUM: 125MG | DIETARY FIBER: 2.4G
TOTAL FAT: 1.6G | TOTAL CARBS: 15.1G | PROTEIN: 12.2G.

Buttery Tofu

This recipe is a vegan take on Butter Chicken, full of spicy flavors this dish is best served with rice and any type of Indian bread.

Servings: 4   Prep Time: 1 Hour plus freezing time   Cook Time: 55 Minutes

Ingredients

1 (19 ounce) block firm tofu
2 tablespoons oil
1/4 teaspoon Salt
2 tablespoons all-purpose flour

FOR THE GRAVY:

3 tablespoons vegan butter
1 teaspoon cumin seeds
1 large onion, chopped
4 cloves garlic, crushed
1 tablespoon fresh ginger, grated
3 ounces tomato paste
1 tablespoon garam masala
1 teaspoon curry powder
1 teaspoon ground coriander
1 teaspoon cayenne pepper
1 teaspoon salt
1 (13 ounce) can coconut milk
Pinch of sugar

Directions

1. Start by placing the tofu in the freezer the day before you wish to use it.
2. When ready to start cooking, remove the tofu from the freezer and defrost in the microwave for approximately 10 minutes. Drain and squeeze the water out of the block. (See Tasty Tofu recipe for instructions of how to squeeze out the liquid)
3. Preheat the oven to 400°F, line a baking sheet with parchment paper.
4. Cut the tofu into bite size cubes, place in a bowl with the oil and salt. Add in the flour and roll the tofu around to make sure it is all coated.
5. Place on the prepared baking sheet and bake in the oven for 30 minutes, turning halfway through. Once cooked set to one side.
6. To make the gravy, melt 3 tablespoons of butter in a large pan over a medium heat.
7. Allow the butter to bubble then add the cumin seeds, cook for approximately one minute.
8. Add in the onions and cook for 5 minutes until softened, then add the garlic, ginger and tomato paste, continue to cook for a couple more minutes.
9. Next add the remaining spices, seasoning and coconut milk. Stir to combine then leave to simmer on a low heat for a further 5 minutes.
10. Remove from the heat then use a stick blender to blend the gravy until lovely and smooth.
11. Add in the baked tofu to the gravy and a pinch of sugar, simmer for a final 5 to 10 minutes.
12. Serve with rice and Indian bread of your choice.

NUTRITIONAL INFO: CALORIES: 441 | SODIUM: 212MG | DIETARY FIBER: 6.1G
TOTAL FAT: 35.6G | TOTAL CARBS: 22.2G | PROTEIN: 16.4G.

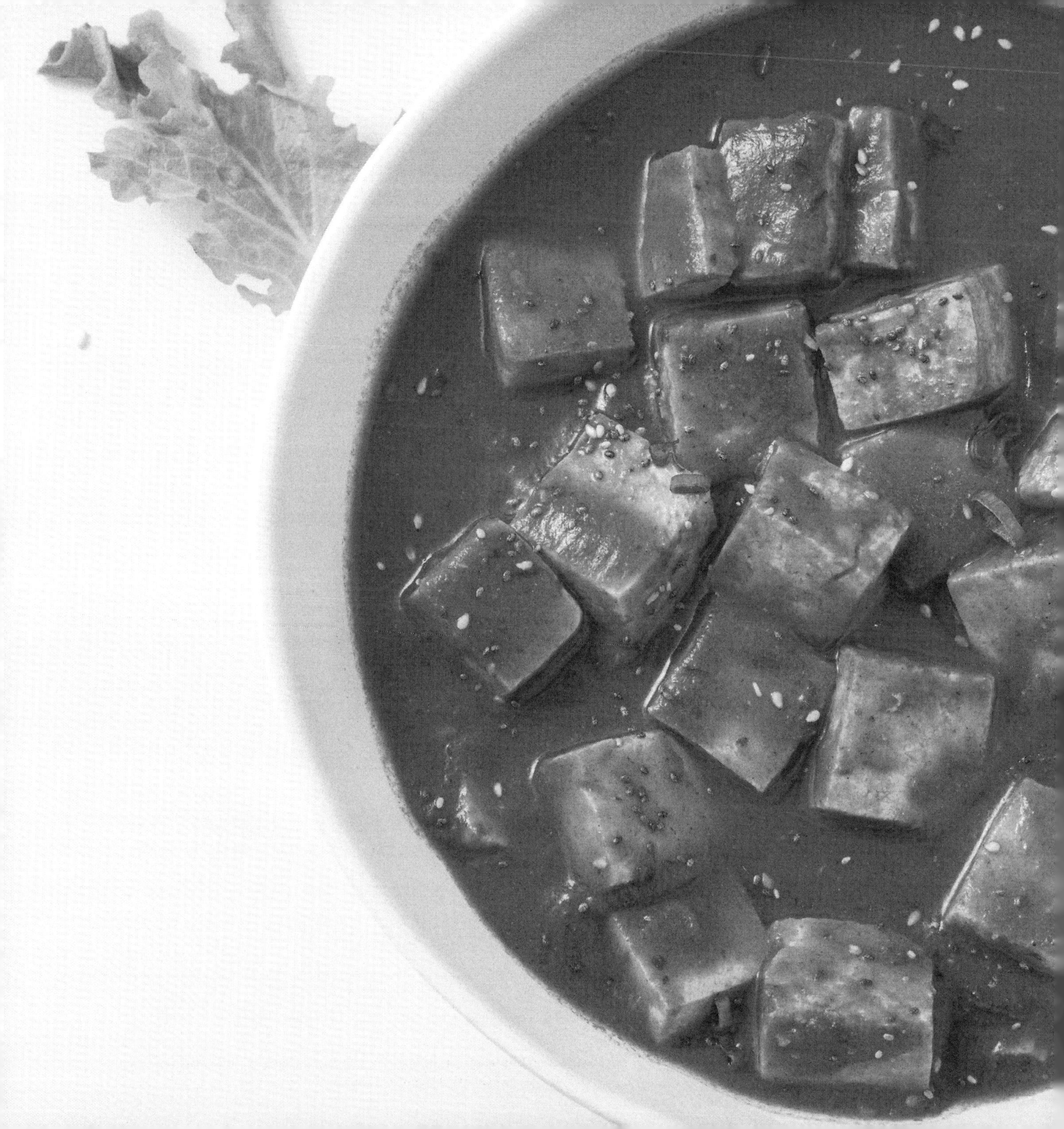

Speedy Stroganoff

When you're in a hurry and need to whip up dinner extra quick - this recipe is just what you need! Serve with rice or noodles to fill up those little tummies!

Servings: 2 people **Prep Time: 5 Minutes** **Cook Time: 10 Minutes**

Ingredients

- 1 tablespoon oil
- 1 medium onion, diced
- 4 cloves garlic, crushed
- 17 1/2 ounces mushrooms, sliced
- 1 teaspoon smoked paprika
- 1/4 cup vegetable stock
- 2 tablespoons sour cream
- Salt and black pepper
- 4 tablespoons fresh parsley, chopped

Directions

1. In a large frying pan, heat the oil over a medium heat, then add in the onion and garlic, cook for 2 to 3 minutes until soft.
2. Put the sliced mushrooms in a bowl, sprinkle over the paprika, then give a good shake so all the mushrooms are covered in the paprika.
3. Add the coated mushrooms to the frying pan and continue to cook for 5 more minutes until the mushrooms are tender and lightly browned.
4. Pour in the stock and sour cream, season, then stir well and simmer until the sauce has thickened a little.
5. Check the seasoning and then sprinkle over the parsley to serve.

NUTRITIONAL INFO: CALORIES: 177 | SODIUM: 196MG | DIETARY FIBER: 4.4G
TOTAL FAT: 10.6G | TOTAL CARBS: 17.1G | PROTEIN: 9.6G.

Salmon and Noodle Stir Fry

Hokkien noodles are so versatile and are great to use when in a hurry. Quick and easy to prepare, they add great texture to this dish.

Servings: 4   Prep Time: 10 Minutes   Cook Time: 15 Minutes

Ingredients

17 ounces wholegrain hokkien noodles
1 clove garlic, crushed
1/3 cup soy sauce
1/4 cup honey
3 tablespoons vegetable oil
12 ounces salmon, cubed
1/2 red pepper, thinly sliced
1 bunch bok choi, chopped
1 zucchini, thinly sliced
2 carrots, thinly sliced
3 spring onions, thinly sliced
2 tablespoons sesame seeds

Directions

1. Start by placing the hokkien noodles in a pan, cover with boiling water, cover with a lid, then leave for 5 minutes. Do not put it on the heat. After 5 minutes they should be soft, so drain off the water and set to one side.
2. In a small bowl, make the sauce by mixing together the garlic, soy sauce and honey.
3. Put a wok on a high heat, add in the oil, then toss in the salmon cubes and fry for a couple of minutes on each side until cooked through. Transfer to a plate.
4. Next, throw in the pepper, bok choi, zucchini and carrots, fry for 2 to 3 minutes, keep moving the veggies around to prevent them from burning.
5. Add in the noodles and the sauce and continue to fry for 5 minutes.
6. Put the salmon back into the wok with the rest of the ingredients and give everything a good shake round to make sure the salmon is coated in the sauce.
7. To serve, sprinkle over the spring onions and sesame seeds.

NUTRITIONAL INFO: CALORIES: 666 | SODIUM: 799MG | DIETARY FIBER: 13.4G
TOTAL FAT: 19.4G | TOTAL CARBS: 109G | PROTEIN: 25.5G.

Chicken Soup

If chicken soup is for the soul, then this recipe is for the heart, soul and tummy - a lovely warming dish to make everyone feel good!

Servings: 6   Prep Time: 15 Minutes   Cook Time: 50 Minutes

Ingredients

- 1 onion, chopped (keep outer layers)
- 3 large carrots, sliced (keep the peel)
- 3 celery stalks, chopped (keep stems and leaves)
- 1 1/2 lbs. chicken thighs
- Salt and pepper to taste
- 1 bay leaf
- 2 tablespoons olive oil
- 3 garlic cloves, crushed
- 1 teaspoon dried oregano
- 3/4 cups vermicelli or other pasta of choice

TO SERVE:

- Parsley for serving
- Lemon juice for serving

Directions

1. Start by cooking the chicken thighs: In a large saucepan, thrown in the scraps from the onion, carrots and celery. Place the chicken thighs on top, then pour over 8 cups of water. Season and add the bay leaf. Next, bring to the boil, then reduce the heat and allow to simmer for around 20 minutes until the chicken is cooked through and tender.
2. Take the chicken out of the pan and shred to pieces, then set to one side.
3. Strain the stock, just keeping the liquid only, then put to one side for later.
4. Using the same saucepan, heat the oil over a medium heat, add the onion and garlic, fry for 2 minutes. Then toss in the celery and carrots. Season with salt, pepper and oregano and cook for 10 minutes until the veggies are soft. Stir from time to time.
5. Return the chicken and the stock to the pan and simmer for a further 10 minutes.
6. Add in the pasta and cook for 5 to 7 minutes until the pasta is al dente.
7. Serve immediately with a sprinkle of parsley and a squeeze of lemon juice.

NUTRITIONAL INFO: CALORIES: 309 | SODIUM: 157MG | DIETARY FIBER: 1.9G
TOTAL FAT: 13.3G | TOTAL CARBS: 11.4G | PROTEIN: 34.4G.

Cheesy Chicken Dippers

Chicken dippers make the perfect finger food - a great, easy midweek meal. Add a side of Zucchini and Baguette Crouton Salad to make this dinner really healthy.

Servings: 4   Prep Time: 10 Minutes   Cook Time: 20 Minutes

Ingredients

2 cups cheese crackers

1/4 teaspoon sea salt

1/4 teaspoon black pepper

2 large eggs

1 teaspoon olive oil

2 chicken breasts, skin removed, sliced into thin strips

FOR DIPPING SAUCE:

1 tablespoon plain greek yogurt

2 tablespoons yellow mustard

2 tablespoons honey

1 teaspoon lemon juice

FOR THE MEAL:

2 carrots, cut into sticks

6 ounces snap peas

Ranch dressing, for dipping

Directions

1. Preheat the oven to 400°F, line a baking sheet with parchment paper.
2. Use a food processor, put in the cheese crackers, salt and pepper, and blitz till the crackers become like breadcrumbs. Pour the cracker crumbs into a shallow sided bowl.
3. In another bowl, whisk the eggs and olive oil together, then season with salt and pepper.
4. Gradually dip the slices of chicken in the egg mix several at a time, then place in the cracker crumb mixture, roll them around till they are well coated.
5. Spread the coated chicken strips out on the prepared baking sheet, then bake in the oven for 15 to 20 minutes, turning halfway through. Bake until golden brown and cooked through.
6. Meanwhile make the mustard dipping sauce by whisking together all the sauce ingredients.
7. Serve along with the carrot sticks, peas and dipping sauces.

NUTRITIONAL INFO: CALORIES: 259 | SODIUM: 486MG | DIETARY FIBER: 0.8G
TOTAL FAT: 12.8G | TOTAL CARBS: 18.3G | PROTEIN: 16.9G.

Sausage Tray Bake

One pan cooking is perfect for any night of the week. This sausage and veg dish is truly heartwarming.

Servings: 6   Prep Time: 20 Minutes   Cook Time: 45 Minutes

Ingredients

2 lbs. red potatoes, cut into eighths

2 cups carrots, cut into large pieces

Olive oil

1-ounce packet ranch dressing powder mix

Black pepper for seasoning

1/2 yellow onion, chopped

1 bell pepper, chopped into large pieces

1 package chicken apple sausage, cut into 1/2-inch rounds

Directions

1. Preheat the oven to 400°F.
2. Place the potatoes and carrots on a baking tray, drizzle over the olive oil, then sprinkle over half of the ranch dressing, season with the pepper. Give the tray a good shake so everything is coated in the oil, ranch dressing and pepper.
3. Place in the oven and bake for 25 minutes.
4. Take the tray out of the oven and add in the onion, bell pepper and sausage.
5. Sprinkle over the rest of the ranch dressing, toss everything together then return to the oven and bake for a further 20 minutes until everything is well cooked through.
6. Serve immediately!

NUTRITIONAL INFO: CALORIES: 170 | SODIUM: 516MG | DIETARY FIBER: 1.5G
TOTAL FAT: 7G | TOTAL CARBS: 9.4G | PROTEIN: 16.3G.

Beef and Linguini Stir-fry

This dish is bursting with mouth-watering flavor. Get a head start by marinating the beef the day before.

Servings: 6   Prep Time: 20 Minutes   Cook Time: 10 Minutes

Ingredients

FOR THE MARINADE:

- 2/3 cups reduced-sodium soy sauce
- 2/3 cups beef broth
- 2 tablespoons brown sugar
- 4 cloves garlic, minced
- 2 teaspoons ginger, minced
- 16 ounces boneless beef sirloin steak, thinly sliced
- 1 teaspoon cornstarch
- 16 ounces linguini noodles
- 4 teaspoons canola oil
- 1 red bell pepper, thinly sliced
- 1 onion, thinly sliced
- 2 carrots, thinly sliced
- 2 cups broccoli florets
- 2 cups cabbage, shredded
- Sesame seeds, to taste
- Red pepper flakes, to taste

Directions

1. Make the marinade by whisking all the marinade ingredients together in a bowl. Split evenly between 2 bowls.
2. Add the slices of beef to one of the bowls of marinade, ensure all the beef is covered in the marinade. Then cover the bowl and place in the refrigerator for a minimum of 2 hours.
3. Add the cornstarch to the second bowl of marinade, mix until smooth then cover and place in the refrigerator for later.
4. Cook the linguini according to the instructions on the package.
5. While the linguini cooks, heat 2 teaspoons of oil in a large frying pan on a medium to high heat, then add in the beef slices and stir-fry for approximately 5 minutes until lightly browned, then remove from the pan and set to one side.
6. Heat the rest of the oil in the pan, then add the peppers, onions, carrots and broccoli and stir-fry until softened.
7. Add the cabbage and beef to the pan and cook until the cabbage is tender.
8. Drain the linguini and toss into the frying pan along with the beef and vegetables then add the marinade and cornstarch mixture. Stir until mixed well.
9. Serve immediately with a sprinkle of sesame seeds and red pepper flakes.

NUTRITIONAL INFO: CALORIES: 404 | SODIUM: 397MG | DIETARY FIBER: 3.4G
TOTAL FAT: 15.2G | TOTAL CARBS: 44G | PROTEIN: 21.4G.

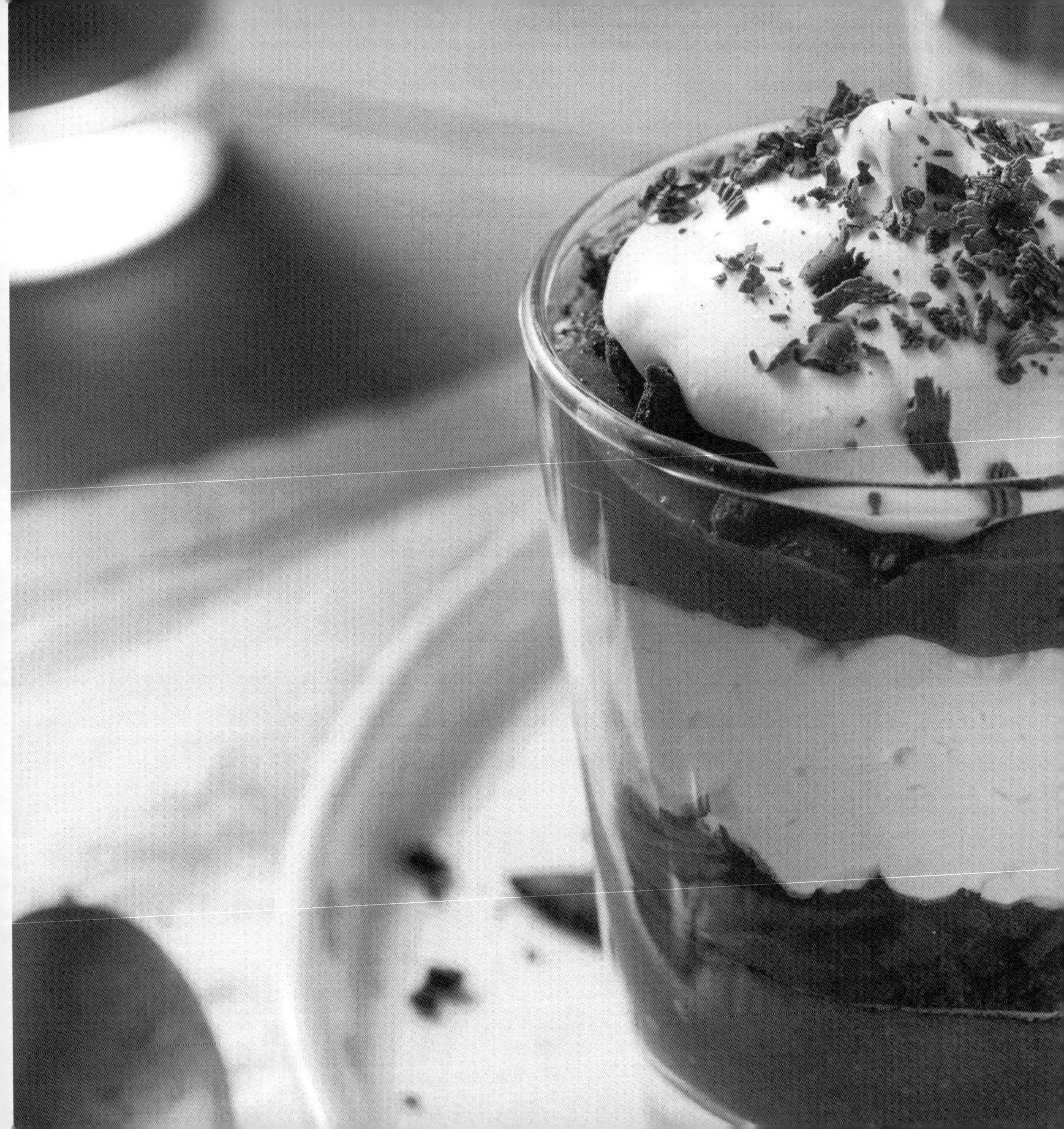

CHAPTER 10
Desserts

Blueberry Crumble

This lovely dessert is best served warm with vanilla ice cream or custard.

Servings: 12   Prep Time: 10 Minutes   Cook Time: 45 Minutes

Ingredients

FRUIT:

3/4 cups sugar

3 tablespoons all-purpose flour

6 cups blueberries

Juice from one lemon

CRUMBLE TOPPING:

3/4 cups all-purpose flour

3/4 cups brown sugar

1/2 cup (1 stick) cold unsalted butter, cubed

1 1/2 cups rolled oats

1/2 teaspoon cinnamon

1/4 teaspoon salt

Directions

1. Preheat the oven to 400°F, grease a 9 x 13-inch ovenproof dish.
2. Make the fruit: Start by mixing together the sugar and flour in a large mixing bowl.
3. Stir in the blueberries and lemon juice, give the bowl a good shake so everything is well combined. Then pour the mixture into the prepared ovenproof dish.
4. Next, make the crumble topping, using a food processor, put in the flour, brown sugar and butter, then use the pulse setting to form a crumb-like mixture.
5. Mix in the oats, cinnamon and salt.
6. Pour the topping mixture over the fruit, making sure it is evenly spread out, then bake in the oven for 40 to 45 minutes until lightly browned.
7. Serve warm.

NUTRITIONAL INFO: CALORIES: 264 | SODIUM: 109MG | DIETARY FIBER: 3.8G
TOTAL FAT: 8.8G | TOTAL CARBS: 45.8G | PROTEIN: 3.2G.

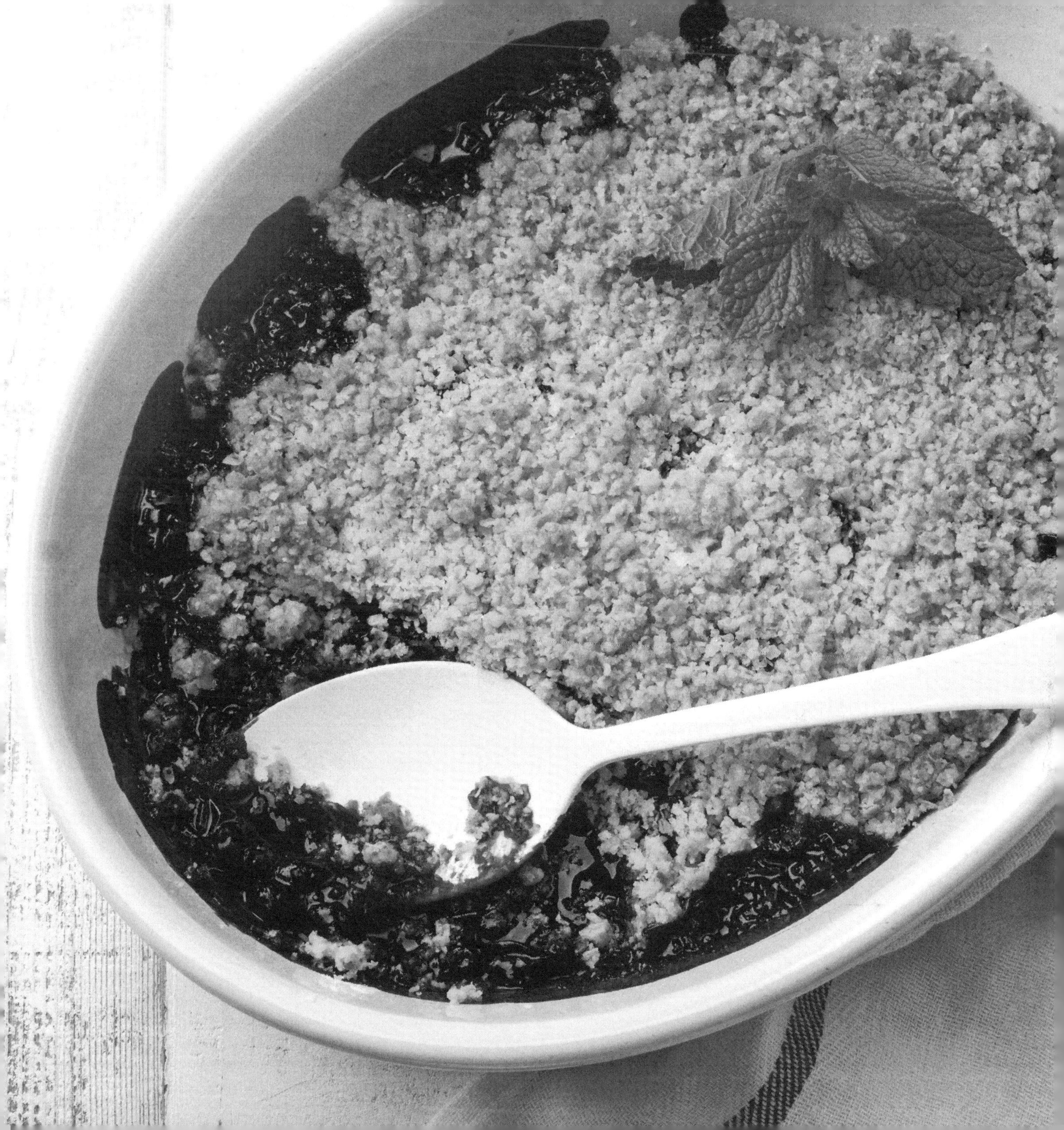

Syrupy Apples

A delicious and healthy warm dessert. Quick and easy to prepare, serve on its own, with a dollop of whipped cream or even with a scoop of ice cream.

Servings: 3   Prep Time: 5 Minutes   Cook Time: 15 Minutes

Ingredients

3 apples, peeled and cubed
2 tablespoons water
1 tablespoon coconut oil
1 tablespoon maple syrup
1/2 teaspoon ground cinnamon
1/8 teaspoon salt
1/4 teaspoon vanilla extract

Directions

1. Place the chopped apple and water in a saucepan, cover with the lid, and cook for 5 minutes over a medium heat until the apples are softened.
2. Stir in the coconut oil and cook for another 5 minutes.
3. Next, mix in the maple syrup, cinnamon, salt and vanilla extract. Continue to cook for a further 5 minutes, while gently stirring.
4. The apples are done once they are fully softened.
5. Serve warm with a dollop of cream.

NUTRITIONAL INFO: CALORIES: 174 | SODIUM: 100MG | DIETARY FIBER: 5.6G
TOTAL FAT: 4.9G | TOTAL CARBS: 35.6G | PROTEIN: 0.6G.

Summer Lollies

Who doesn't love a berry lolly? These summer lollies are perfectly refreshing on a hot day!

Servings: 6 to 8 Lollies   **Prep Time: 10 Minutes plus freezing time**   **Cook Time: None**

Ingredients

1 1/2 cups vanilla Greek yogurt

2 cups mixed fresh berries

1 tablespoon honey

EQUIPMENT:

Ice lolly molds and sticks

Directions

1. Using a blender, place the yoghurt, berries and honey inside, then blend until smooth.

2. Pour the mixture into the ice lolly molds, pop in the sticks, then freeze for 6 to 8 hours until firm.

3. To serve, run the mold under cold water for a few seconds, this will help to loosen the mold and help the frozen lolly to come out easier.

NUTRITIONAL INFO: CALORIES: 40 | SODIUM: 14MG | DIETARY FIBER: 0.5G
TOTAL FAT: 0.1G | TOTAL CARBS: 7G | PROTEIN: 2.8G.

Peach and Blueberry Bake

Save any leftovers for the next day and enjoy cold with porridge for a healthy breakfast.

Servings: 4   Prep Time: 5 Minutes   Cook Time: 25 Minutes

Ingredients

4 peaches, peeled and sliced
1 1/2 cups fresh blueberries
1/8 teaspoon ground cinnamon
3 tablespoons brown sugar

Directions

1. Preheat the oven to 350°F, prepare an ovenproof baking dish.
2. Place the peach slices and blueberries evenly across the base of the ovenproof dish.
3. Mix the cinnamon and brown sugar together in a small bowl then sprinkle over the fruit.
4. Bake in the oven for 20 minutes, then change the setting to a medium broil and cook for a further 5 minutes until bubbling.
5. Cool slightly then serve.

NUTRITIONAL INFO: CALORIES: 90 | SODIUM: 1MG | DIETARY FIBER: 3.7G
TOTAL FAT: 0.6G | TOTAL CARBS: 24.3G | PROTEIN: 1.8G.

Refrigerator Cheesecake

Want to impress with a great dessert but don't have time to bake? Here's a nifty little cheesecake that will definitely dazzle!

Servings: 4   Prep Time: 15 Minutes plus setting time   Cook Time: None

Ingredients

1 1/2 cups graham cracker crumbs
6 tablespoons butter, melted
4 ounces cream cheese, softened
3 tablespoons granulated sugar
4 ounces frozen whipped topping, thawed
Assorted fruit, sliced

Directions

1. Prepare the base: Mix the graham cracker crumbs and the melted butter together in a bowl, once well combined, pour into a flan dish. Use your fingers to spread the crumb mix evenly over the base of the dish then press down firmly to make a solid base.
2. In another bowl, whisk together the cream cheese, sugar and whipped topping until well combined.
3. Pour the cream cheese mixture over the base and smooth out using a palette knife.
4. Place in the refrigerator and allow to set for 2 to 3 hours.
5. Before serving, decorate with the sliced assorted fruit.

Strawberries and Cream Shortcake

This classic dessert is the definition of summer! A real treat that will bring a smile to everyone's face!

Servings: 12　　**Prep Time: 1 Hour 15 Minutes**　　**Cook Time: 15 Minutes**

Ingredients

STRAWBERRY TOPPING:

5 lbs. strawberries, hulled and quartered
1 cup granulated sugar

BISCUITS:

2 1/2 cups all-purpose flour
2 tablespoons baking powder
2 teaspoons granulated sugar
1 teaspoon salt
1/2 cup cold unsalted butter, cubed
1 cup cold buttermilk
1/4 cup unsalted butter, melted

CREAM TOPPING:

1 1/2 cups heavy cream
4 1/2 teaspoons granulated sugar
1 teaspoon vanilla extract
1 teaspoon powdered sugar, for dusting

Directions

1. Start by softening the strawberries: In a large bowl, mix together the strawberries and sugar, then leave for 5 minutes.
2. Using a potato masher, carefully squash the strawberries a little to open them up a bit, then put them to one side for an hour to continue to soften.
3. Next make the biscuits: Preheat the oven to 425°F, line a large baking tray with parchment paper.
4. Mix the flour, baking powder, sugar and salt together in a bowl. Then add in the cubes of butter, use your fingertips to rub the butter into the flour mixture until it resembles breadcrumbs.
5. Make a well in the center of the flour and butter mixture, pour the buttermilk into the well, then using a spatula gradually bring the mixture together until it forms a sticky dough.
6. Flour your hands and the work surface, then transfer the dough to the surface and gently fold the dough, being careful not to knead the dough, but just stretch slightly and fold it a few times.
7. Then use a rolling pin, roll the dough to 1/2-inch thickness, choose a small round cookie cutter to cut out the biscuit then place on the baking tray, use all the dough to cut out 24 biscuits.
8. Lightly brush the rounds with melted butter and bake for 10 to 15 minutes until lightly browned. Place on a wire rack to cool.
9. Meanwhile make the cream: Whisk together the cream, granulated sugar and vanilla extract until the cream has thickened and forms soft peaks.
10. Finally assemble the dessert: Place 12 biscuits on a plate to form the bases, then pile a tablespoonful of strawberries on the biscuit bases, top with a dollop of cream then carefully balance another biscuit on the top. Place the teaspoon of powdered sugar in a sieve then dust over the tops of the biscuits.
11. Serve and enjoy!

NUTRITIONAL INFO: CALORIES: 330 | SODIUM: 275MG | DIETARY FIBER: 4.5G
TOTAL FAT: 12.5G | TOTAL CARBS: 53.2G | PROTEIN: 4.8G.

Not So Foolish Fool!

This recipe uses crushed strawberries, but you can substitute any fruit according to the season or what you have at home.

Servings: 4   Prep Time: 20 minutes plus setting time   Cook Time: None

Ingredients

1 cup heavy cream

2 cups fresh strawberries, hulled

1 tablespoon sugar

1 teaspoon vanilla extract

A few extra strawberries, sliced, to garnish

Directions

1. Whisk the cream until it is thick and forms soft peaks. Place in the refrigerator for later.
2. Quarter the strawberries then place in a bowl and sprinkle over the sugar and vanilla extract, allow to stand for a few minutes.
3. Next, roughly mash the strawberries so some are crushed but keep some bigger pieces too. Set to one side for 10 minutes.
4. Gently fold half the crushed strawberries into the cream.
5. To serve: In four sundae glasses, layer spoonful of cream mixture, then crushed strawberries, then cream mixture, until all the cream and crushed strawberries are used up, finishing with a cream layer at the top.
6. Decorate the top with a couple of slices of strawberries.
7. Refrigerate for 30 minutes, then serve.

NUTRITIONAL INFO: CALORIES: 141 | SODIUM: 12MG | DIETARY FIBER: 1.4G
TOTAL FAT: 11.3G | TOTAL CARBS: 9.5G | PROTEIN: 1.1G.

Banana Cake Squares

Comfort food warning! These yummy squares will soon disappear!

Servings: 16 Squares**Prep Time: 25 Minutes****Cook Time: 18 Minutes**

Ingredients

1 cup mashed ripe banana

1/3 cup coconut sugar

3 tablespoons unsalted butter, melted

2 tablespoons milk

1 large egg

1 teaspoon vanilla extract

3/4 cups all-purpose flour

1/2 teaspoon baking soda

1/2 teaspoon ground cinnamon

1/8 teaspoon ground nutmeg

1/4 teaspoon salt

1/3 cup plus 2 tablespoons dark chocolate chips, divided

Directions

1. Preheat the oven to 350°F, line and grease an 8 x 8-inch baking pan.
2. In a large mixing bowl, combine the mashed banana, coconut sugar, melted butter, milk, egg and vanilla extract. Stir well.
3. In another bowl, mix the flour, baking soda, cinnamon, nutmeg, and salt together.
4. Next, fold the flour mixture into the banana mixture. Mix to ensure fully combined.
5. Stir in the 1/3 cup chocolate chips.
6. Pour the batter into the baking pan, smooth out with a palette knife so that the batter is evenly spread over the whole pan.
7. Scatter over the 2 tablespoons of chocolate chips, then bake in the oven to 18 to 20 minutes until firm to touch and nicely browned on top.
8. Turn out onto a wire rack to cool, then cut into squares to serve.

NUTRITIONAL INFO: CALORIES: 87 | SODIUM: 88MG | DIETARY FIBER: 0.6G
TOTAL FAT: 3.3G | TOTAL CARBS: 13.8G | PROTEIN: 1.4G.

Very Berry Cheesecakes

None-baked cheesecake can tend to fall apart when you serve it, so making individual cheesecakes is a great way to avoid all that mess!

Servings: 8 **Prep Time: 20 Minutes plus setting time** **Cook Time: None**

Ingredients

16 ounces fresh strawberries, hulled and sliced

6 ounces fresh raspberries

1 teaspoon granulated sugar

BASE:

9 rectangular graham crackers, crushed into fine crumbs

1 tablespoon granulated sugar

4 tablespoons butter, melted

CHEESECAKE TOPPING:

16 ounces light cream cheese, softened

1/2 cup powdered sugar

1 teaspoon fresh lemon juice

1/2 teaspoon vanilla extract

1 cup low fat vanilla Greek yogurt

Directions

1. Mix the strawberries, raspberries and sugar together in a bowl. Stir to combine, then set to the side for 15 minutes so the berries soften.

2. Meanwhile, make the base by mixing together the crushed crackers, sugar and melted butter. Once combined, divide the base mixture between 8 sundae or trifle dishes. Press gently into the base of each dish.

3. Next, make the cheesecake topping by beating the cream cheese and powdered sugar together in a bowl for 2 to 3 minutes until it becomes a light, creamy texture.

4. Add in the lemon juice, vanilla extract and Greek yogurt, continue to beat for another minute.

5. To assemble: Line up the 8 dishes with the bases in. Then layer a spoonful of the strawberry and raspberry mixture on the bases, followed by a spoonful of the cream cheese mixture, then finish with a layer of berries.

6. Place in the refrigerator for 30 minutes or until ready to serve.

NUTRITIONAL INFO: CALORIES: 228 | SODIUM: 222MG | DIETARY FIBER: 3.6G
TOTAL FAT: 9.5G | TOTAL CARBS: 35.5G | PROTEIN: 3G.

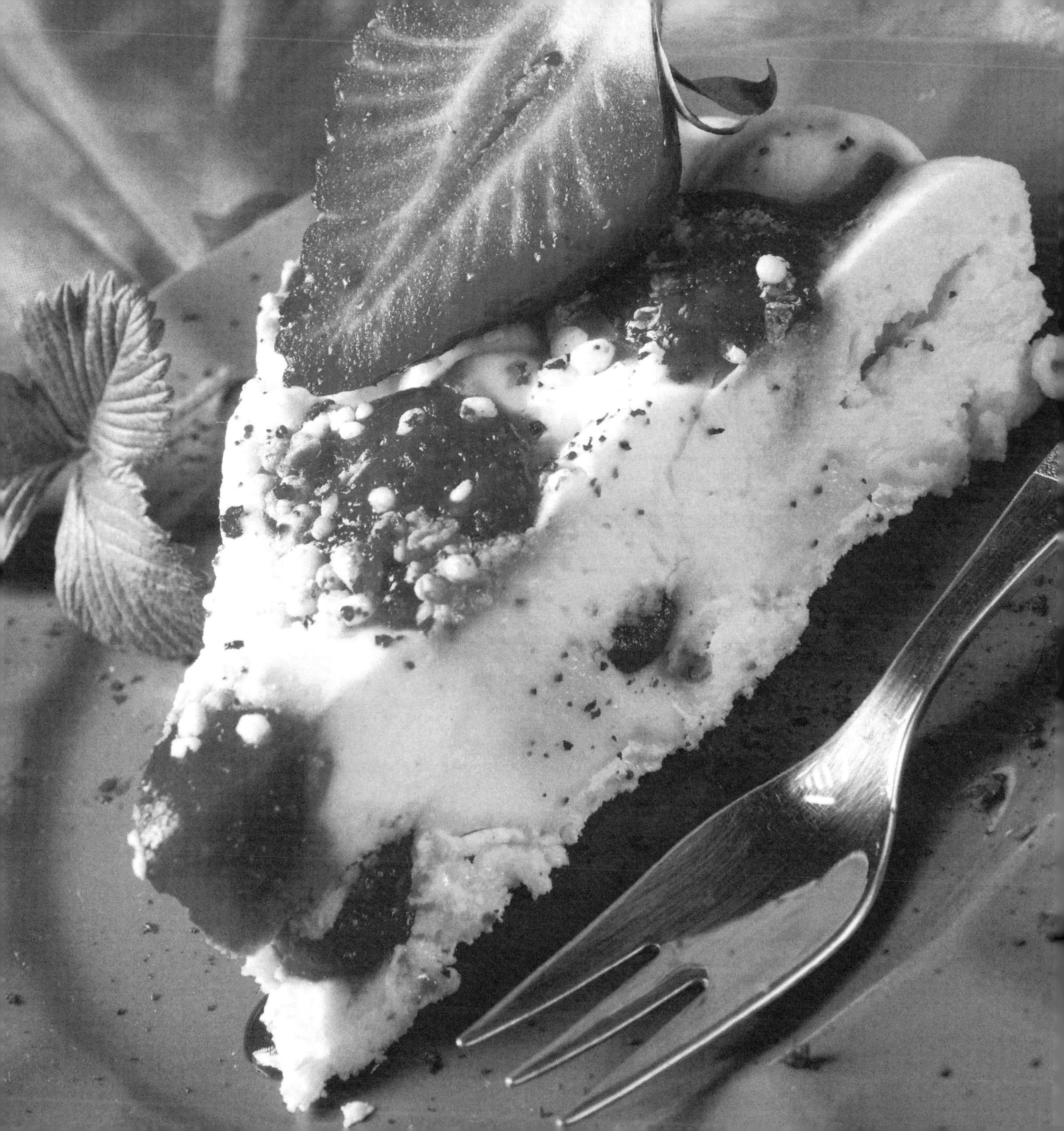

Nutty Coconut Ice Cream

A wonderful combination of fruit, ice cream, nuts and cocoa, this dessert is healthy and vegan. Make it gluten free by replacing the oats with buckwheat groats.

Servings: 6   Prep Time: 15 Minutes plus freezing time   Cook Time: None

Ingredients

2 cups mixed fresh fruit

ICE CREAM:

1 can raw coconut milk
1/4 cup raw cane sugar
1 banana, mashed

BASE:

1/3 cup walnuts
1/3 cup raw oats
2 tablespoons cacao powder
2/3 cups dates

Directions

1. Line a deep sided cake pan with saran wrap, then cover the sides with the mixed fruit.
2. Make the ice cream by whisking the coconut milk, cane sugar and mashed banana together.
3. Pour the mixture into the cake pan with the fruit, then place in the freezer for 3 to 4 hours until solid.
4. Next make the base: Use a food processor, add in the walnuts, oats and cocoa, pulse until fine and flour-like.
5. Put in the dates and continue to pulse until it forms a sticky paste.
6. Spread the date mixture over the top of the ice cream, then refrigerate for an hour until set.
7. Turn out the dessert onto a plate, the date mixture forming the base. Remove the plastic wrap, allow to thaw slightly before serving.

NUTRITIONAL INFO: CALORIES: 306 | SODIUM: 10MG | DIETARY FIBER: 6.2G
TOTAL FAT: 15.4G | TOTAL CARBS: 45.7G | PROTEIN: 5.2G.

Aussie Pavlova

Sweet, creamy and fruity - simply delicious!

Servings: 8   Prep Time: 20 Minutes   Cook Time: 1 Hour

Ingredients

6 egg whites
1/8 teaspoon cream of tartar
1 1/2 cups caster sugar
2 teaspoons vanilla extract
2 cups heavy cream
1 tablespoon powdered sugar
2 cups berries or sliced fruit
2 teaspoons lemon zest
1 tablespoon golden syrup

Directions

1. Preheat the oven to 250°F, line a baking sheet with parchment paper.
2. Place the egg whites in a large (non-plastic) bowl, either using a hand-held electric whisk or a stand mixer, beat on a medium speed until starting to froth then add in a pinch of salt and 1 teaspoon of the vanilla extract, continue to beat until the egg whites stand in stiff peaks.
3. Turn up the whisk/ mixer speed and gradually add in a spoonful of sugar at a time, continue to beat until the mixture is thick and glossy. Add in the cream of tartar and beat for one more minute.
4. Carefully tip the meringue out of the bowl onto the prepared baking sheet, use a palette knife to make it into a round shape with a well in the center.
5. Place in the oven and bake for one hour until firm to touch. Turn off the oven and open the door slightly, allow the meringue to cool in the oven.
6. Meanwhile whisk the cream, powdered sugar and remaining vanilla together till it forms soft peaks.
7. Once cooled, place the meringue on a serving plate and start the assembly: First cover the meringue with the whipped cream, then spoon over the berries or fruit, finish with a sprinkle of lemon zest and lastly a drizzle of syrup.
8. Serve and enjoy!

NUTRITIONAL INFO: CALORIES: 292 | SODIUM: 40MG | DIETARY FIBER: 1.3G
TOTAL FAT: 11.3G | TOTAL CARBS: 46G | PROTEIN: 3.6G.

Super Fruity Fruit Salad

Packed with fresh flavor this healthy dessert is a real treat for the body! Enjoy it on its own or with a dollop of whipped cream.

Servings: 18   Prep Time: 10 Minutes   Cook Time: 5 Minutes

Ingredients

1/2 cup orange juice

1 teaspoon orange zest, grated

1/4 cup lemon juice

1 teaspoon lemon zest, grated

1/4 cup honey

1 teaspoon vanilla extract

3 cups strawberries, halved

4 tangerines, segmented

3 cups pineapple chunks

3 kiwis, peeled and sliced

2 cups blueberries

2 cups red grapes

Mint to garnish

Directions

1. Start by making the fruit syrup: In a saucepan, place orange juice, orange zest, lemon juice, lemon zest and honey. Slowly bring to the boil whilst whisking. Once the mixture has boiled add in the vanilla extract, whisk again, then turn off the heat and leave to cool.

2. Place all the prepared fruit in a large serving bowl, pour over the cooled syrup, then mix well.

3. Garnish with mint and serve!

NUTRITIONAL INFO: CALORIES: 83 | SODIUM: 2MG | DIETARY FIBER: 2.5G
TOTAL FAT: 0.3G | TOTAL CARBS: 21G | PROTEIN: 1.1G.

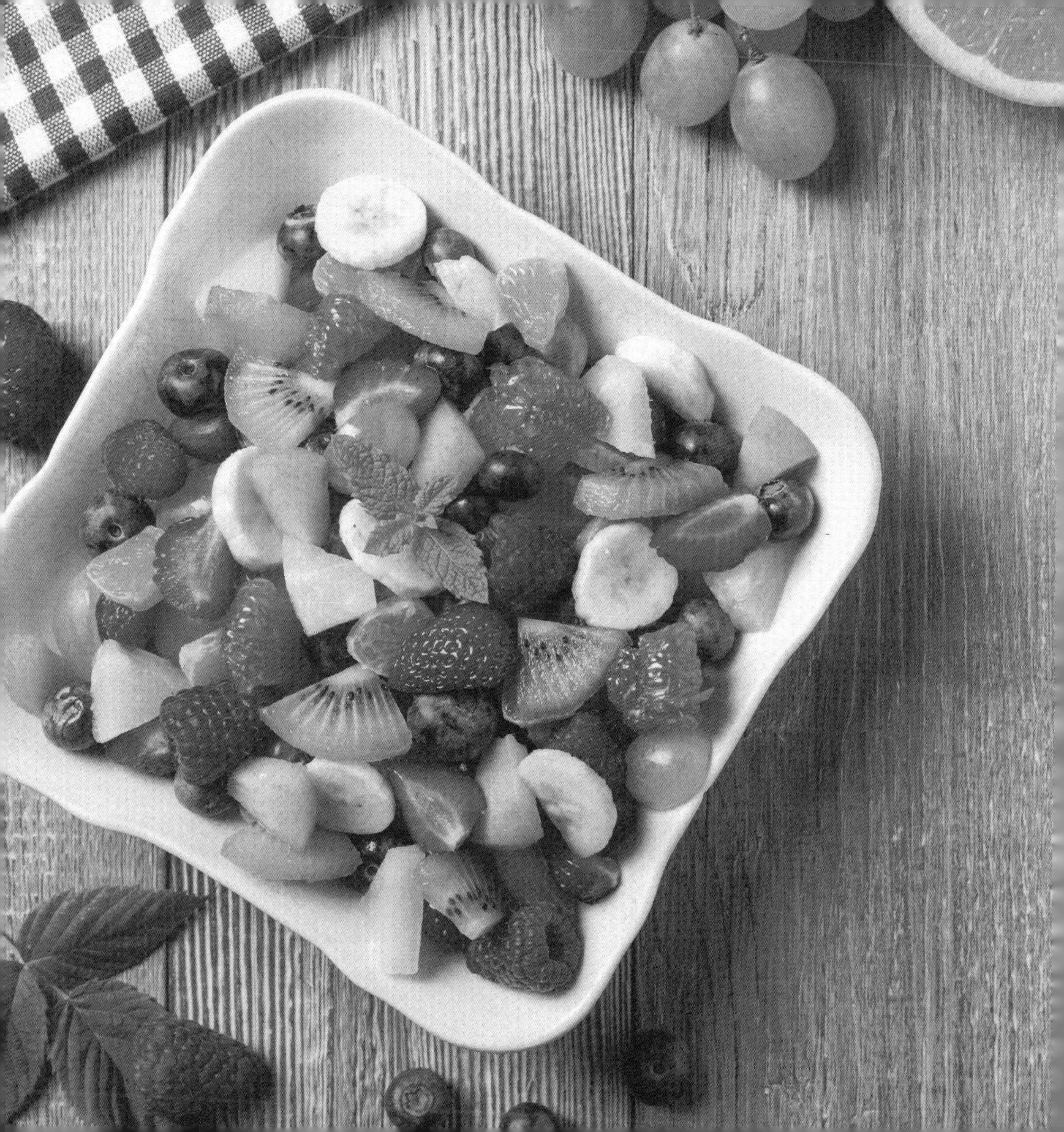

Cold Fruit Custard

Creamy custard is delicious either warm or cold. Serving it cold with fruit is a wonderful indulgence!

Servings: 4   Prep Time: 5 Minutes plus chilling time   Cook Time: 20 Minutes

Ingredients

3 tablespoons custard powder
5 tablespoons sugar
3 1/4 cups whole milk
2 cups mixed fruits, sliced

Directions

1. Put the custard powder and sugar in a small bowl, pour in 1/4 cup milk and stir quickly to combine, keep stirring until you have a smooth paste.
2. Pour the rest of the milk into a saucepan, add in the custard powder and sugar paste, stir continuously while very slowly bringing to a simmer.
3. Once the custard has started to thicken, take it off the heat and cover with plastic wrap then place in the fridge to cool for 2 hours.
4. To serve: stir the fruit into the cooled custard and divide between individual serving bowls.

NUTRITIONAL INFO: CALORIES: 316 | SODIUM: 83MG | DIETARY FIBER: 2.4G
TOTAL FAT: 6.7G | TOTAL CARBS: 59.1G | PROTEIN: 8.2G.

Panna Cotta with Passion

It can be very tempting to turn up the heat to speed things up but keep the temperature low and take your time - you'll be rewarded with perfect Panna Cotta!

Servings: 12 Small portions **Prep Time: 30 Minutes plus setting time** **Cook Time: None**

Ingredients

- 1/4 cup whole milk
- 1 1/2 teaspoons unflavored gelatin
- 1 1/2 cups heavy cream
- 2/3 cups granulated sugar
- 1 teaspoon vanilla extract or vanilla paste
- 1 cup sour cream
- 1/2 cup passion fruit puree, without seeds

Directions

1. Pour the milk into a saucepan, sprinkle over the gelatin then stir. Leave to stand for 2 minutes.
2. Put the pan on a low heat and stir until the gelatin has dissolved.
3. Add in 1/2 cup of cream and continue to heat and stir.
4. Once it is steaming, but not boiling, add the sugar and continue stirring until fully dissolved.
5. Next, gradually pour in 1 cup cream while whisking the mixture.
6. Add in the vanilla and sour cream and continue to whisk until smooth and thickened.
7. Add in the passion fruit puree, mix well then remove from the heat.
8. Divide the mixture between 12 small cups, glasses or bowls, then refrigerate for 3 to 4 hours until set.

NUTRITIONAL INFO: CALORIES: 151 | SODIUM: 22MG | DIETARY FIBER: 1G
TOTAL FAT: 9.8G | TOTAL CARBS: 14.9G | PROTEIN: 2.1G.

Chocolate Trifle

This is one for the chocolate lover - decadent, delicious and dangerously good!

Servings: 8   Prep Time: 20 Minutes   Cook Time: 30 Minutes

Ingredients

- 7 ounces unsweetened chocolate, roughly chopped
- 3/4 cups unsalted butter
- 1/4 cup water
- 1 cup caster sugar
- 3/4 cups light brown sugar
- 2 large eggs
- 1 teaspoon vanilla extract
- 1 1/3 cups all-purpose flour
- 1/8 teaspoon salt
- 4 cups raspberries
- Mini chocolate chips, to garnish

CREAM TOPPING:

- 1 1/2 cups heavy cream
- 1/3 cup sour cream
- 3 tablespoons sugar
- 2 teaspoons vanilla extract

Directions

1. Preheat the oven to 350ºF. Grease and line a 9 x 12-inch baking pan.
2. Place the chocolate, butter and water in a saucepan, put on a low heat and gently melt the chocolate and butter, stirring continuously.
3. Once melted, pour into a mixing bowl, then add the both sugars, whisk till slightly frothy.
4. Add in the eggs and vanilla extract and continue to whisk for a couple of minutes.
5. Fold in the flour and salt, ensuring all ingredients are well combined, but being careful not to knock out all the air.
6. Pour the batter into the prepared baking pan, ensuring it is evenly spread out across the base of the pan. Place in the oven and bake for 25 minutes. To check if it is cooked, insert a toothpick in the middle of the brownie, if it comes out clean it is done.
7. Leave the brownie in the pan until cool, then tip onto a board and slice into small bite size squares.
8. Next make the whipped cream: pour the heavy cream, sour cream, sugar and vanilla extract into a bowl and use an electric whisk to whisk until thick and standing in soft peaks.
9. To assemble: Line up 8 glass dessert bowls, place a couple of brownie pieces in the bottom, then layer with cream and raspberries, repeat the layers till the bowl is full, then garnish with chocolate chips and serve.

NUTRITIONAL INFO: CALORIES: 651 | SODIUM: 80MG | DIETARY FIBER: 8.7G
TOTAL FAT: 42.4G | TOTAL CARBS: 70.3G | PROTEIN: 8.6G.

Raspberry Layer Cake

Layers of cake, jam and fruit, topped off with heavenly frosting - a real crowd pleaser of a dessert!

Servings: 12 **Prep Time: 15 Minutes plus setting time** **Cook Time: None**

Ingredients

2 ounces cream cheese, softened

3 tablespoons powdered sugar

1 cup heavy cream

1/4 teaspoon vanilla extract

1 frozen all-butter pound cake, defrosted

1/2 cup lemon curd

2 cups raspberries

3 tablespoons raspberry jam

Directions

1. Start by making the frosting, place the cream cheese and sugar in a mixing bowl and beat until smooth.
2. Pour in the cream and vanilla extract and continue to beat until it forms stiff peaks, place in the refrigerator until required.
3. Place the pound cake on its side, then cut horizontally into 3 long slices (base, middle and top)
4. Place the base piece on a serving plate and spread with half of the lemon curd, then layer with 3/4 cup raspberries.
5. Take the middle slice of cake, spread half the jam on one side, then place on top of the raspberries, jam side down.
6. Next, spread the middle cake layer with the remaining lemon curd and another layer of raspberries.
7. Spread the remaining jam on the underside of the top slice of cake then place on top.
8. Carefully spread the frosting over the sides and top of the cake, then place in the refrigerator for at least 2 hours.
9. Before serving, decorate the top with the remaining raspberries, slice and enjoy.

NUTRITIONAL INFO: CALORIES: 133 | SODIUM: 80MG | DIETARY FIBER: 1.4G
TOTAL FAT: 10G | TOTAL CARBS: 12.2G | PROTEIN: 1.7G.

Speedy Sorbet

Get a head start on this recipe by having a bottle of sugar syrup prepared in the fridge and different fruits stored in bags in the freezer, then just weigh out what you need and away you go!

N.B. Use agave nectar, maple syrup or orange juice as substitutes for the sugar syrup.

Servings: 4   Prep Time: 15 Minutes plus freezing time   Cook Time: None

Ingredients

SUGAR SYRUP:

8 ounces caster sugar
2 cups water

RASPBERRY SORBET:

8 ounces raspberries
3 tablespoons sugar syrup
2 teaspoons lemon juice

PINEAPPLE SORBET:

8 ounces pineapple, cubed
3 tablespoons sugar syrup

PEACH SORBET:

8 ounces peaches, peeled and cubed
3 tablespoons sugar syrup
2 teaspoons lemon juice

HONEYDEW MELON SORBET:

8 ounces honeydew melon, cubed
3 tablespoons sugar syrup
l2 teaspoons lemon juice

Directions

1. Start by making the sugar syrup, place the sugar and water in a medium sized saucepan, stir well and heat gently until the sugar has dissolved.
2. Increase the heat slightly and bring the mixture to a simmer. Simmer for 20 minutes until thickened and syrupy. Allow to cool, then chill until needed.
3. To make the sorbet, make sure your fruit is cut into small cubes. Line a baking sheet with parchment paper, then arrange the fruit in a single layer on the sheet. Place in the freezer and leave until the fruit is fully frozen.
4. Place the frozen fruit in a food processor, use the pulse setting and pulse a couple of times, then a tablespoonful at a time, add in the sugar syrup while continuing to pulse.
5. Add in the lemon juice and pulse until smooth.
6. Serve and enjoy!

NUTRITIONAL INFO: CALORIES: 291 | SODIUM: 15MG | DIFTARY FIBER: 3.7G
TOTAL FAT: 0.4G | TOTAL CARBS: 76.1G | PROTEIN: 0.7G.

Chunky Compote

Use whichever combination of fruit you enjoy, plus to make it easier use frozen fruit, just cook it for a few minutes longer.

Servings: 2 cups   Prep Time: 5 Minutes   Cook Time: 10 to 15 Minutes

Ingredients

1 lb. fresh strawberries, peaches and frozen blueberries

2 tablespoons honey or maple syrup

1/4 cup water

Pinch of salt

Directions

1. Cut the strawberries and peaches into thin slices. Leave the blueberries whole.
2. Place the fruit, honey or maple syrup, water and salt in a saucepan, stirring from time to time, slowly bring to a boil.
3. Reduce the heat and allow to simmer for 5 to 10 minutes until the fruit is softened.
4. Serve immediately or chilled.

NUTRITIONAL INFO: CALORIES: 104 | SODIUM: 3MG | DIETARY FIBER: 2.2G
TOTAL FAT: 0.3G | TOTAL CARBS: 27.1G | PROTEIN: 0.9G.

Brazilian Inspired Mousse

The sweet, tangy taste of passion fruit will bring back memories of the best beach holidays!

Servings: 4   Prep Time: 10 Minutes plus setting time   Cook Time: 10 Minutes

Ingredients

2 teaspoons unflavored gelatin

3 tablespoons water

1 1/3 cups heavy cream

1 (14 ounce) can sweetened condensed milk

1 cup passion fruit pulp

SAUCE:

Pulp of two fresh passion fruits, with seeds

1/4 cup sugar

Directions

1. Place the gelatin in a small bowl, mix in the water, then microwave for 20 seconds so the gelatin melts. Allow to cool slightly.
2. Place the cream, sweetened condensed milk, passion fruit pulp and cooled gelatin in a large bowl and use an electric handheld whisk to mix for 3 to 4 minutes until thickened.
3. Pour into 4 dessert bowls, then place in the refrigerator for 3 hours until set.
4. Meanwhile make the sauce by placing the passion fruit pulp in a saucepan, add the sugar.
5. Slowly bring to a boil, while stirring continuously, then reduce the heat and simmer for 2 minutes until syrupy. Leave to cool.
6. To serve: pour a little cooled sauce over the top of each mousse.

NUTRITIONAL INFO: CALORIES: 482 | SODIUM: 147MG | DIETARY FIBER: 6.1G
TOTAL FAT: 22.8G | TOTAL CARBS: 62.5G | PROTEIN: 10.5G.

Rich Fruit Loaves

Full of fragrant fruit, this heavy fruit cake makes for a super afternoon treat along with a lovely cup of tea!

Servings: 2 Loaves   Prep Time: 30 Minutes plus 1 day to soak the fruit   Cook Time: 1 Hour 30 Mins

Ingredients

FRUIT MIXTURE:

- 1 1/4 cups dark raisins
- 1 1/4 cups golden raisins
- 1 cup dried peaches, chopped
- 1 cup dried apricots, chopped
- 1 cup dried unsweetened black figs, chopped
- 1 cup dried unsweetened tart cherries, chopped
- 3/4 cups dried unsweetened prunes, chopped
- 3/4 cups orange juice

CAKE:

- 1 1/2 cups all-purpose flour
- 1/2 teaspoon baking powder
- 1 teaspoon ground cinnamon
- 1 teaspoon ground ginger
- 1/4 teaspoon ground nutmeg
- 1 teaspoon salt
- 1 stick unsalted butter, softened
- 3/4 cups light brown sugar
- 5 large eggs
- 1 tablespoon orange zest, grated
- 1 tablespoon lemon zest, grated
- 1/2 cup freshly squeezed orange juice
- 1 Granny Smith apple, peeled and grated
- 3/4 cup slivered almonds
- 3 tablespoons crystallized ginger, finely diced

GLAZE:

- 1/4 cup apricot preserve
- 1/4 cup water
- Whole pecans, for garnishing

Directions

1. Place all the dried fruit in a large bowl, pour over the orange juice and mix well. Cover with saran wrap, then leave for 12 to 24 hours at room temperature.
2. Preheat the oven to 300°F, grease two 9 x 5 loaf pans and line with parchment paper.
3. Combine all the dry cake ingredients together in a bowl.
4. In a separate mixing bowl, cream the butter and sugar until light and fluffy
5. Add in the eggs, one at a time and beat well. Add a tablespoonful of the flour mixture if the batter looks like it is starting to curdle.
6. Sieve the dry ingredients over the batter, then fold in gently.
7. Carefully stir in the orange and lemon zests, orange juice, grated apple, almonds, candied ginger, mix well.
8. Add the soaked dried fruit mixture then mix well again until fully combined. The mixture will be thick and heavy.
9. Divide the mixture between the two prepared loaf pans.
10. Bake in the oven for 1 1/2 hours until browned on top and cooked all the way through.
11. Leave to cool in the pan for a few minutes, then turn out onto a wire rack to finish cooling.
12. Prepare the apricot glaze: place the apricot preserve in a small saucepan over a medium heat and pour over the water. Stir to combine.
13. Continue to stir while bringing the mixture to a simmer, stir until shiny and thin enough to glaze the loaves.
14. Brush the loaves with the glaze then decorate with the pecans.
15. Serve slices on their own or lightly buttered.

NUTRITIONAL INFO: CALORIES: 459 | SODIUM: 284MG | DIETARY FIBER: 5.3G
TOTAL FAT: 13.3G | TOTAL CARBS: 73.8G | PROTEIN: 7.8G.

Next Steps...

As you can see, making sure your toddler eats a healthy, nutritional meal every day doesn't need to be a struggle or extra effort, and can even be a learning opportunity. Thank you for buying this book, and may you have wonderful, delicious meal times together with your precious little one and the rest of your family.

Printed in Great Britain
by Amazon